I Am Terezin

With Memory
Comes Responsibility

R. B.

I Am Terezin

A Memoir

by

Richard D. Bank

Auctus Publishers

Havertown, Pennsylvania, United States

I Am Terezin

A Memoir

by Richard D. Bank, ghostwriter

Published by Auctus Publishers, LLC
606 Merion Avenue, First Floor
Havertown, PA 19083, USA

Softcover Edition: ISBN: 978-0-9979607-2-3
Electronic Edition: ISBN: 978-0-9979607-3-0

In memory of Sophie and Ludwig Frank (Theresienstadt 1942-1945)
In honor of their great-great-grandchildren, Hayden and Rebecca Bank
And, as always, for Frani.

Foreword

Richard Bank's "I Am Terezin" is as captivating as it is compelling a book that looks at the tortured history and conflicting personality of the infamous so-called "Paradise Ghetto" but through the eyes of the concentration camp, itself. In prose that is both poetic and pitiful, the ghostwriter escorts the reader on a very personal journey of unrelenting anguish and torment. Time and again, this "memoir" refers to the forlorn and forsaken Jewish inmates of the camp as "my people," evoking a wrenching, aching desire to want to somehow alleviate their unbearable suffering but, alas, to no avail.

Terezin adopts a self-reflective attitude on many an occasion: "I never slept so I was aware of everything that went on within me at every moment in time....so long as even one of my inhabitants had eyes open and did not sleep...I too would be awake...The nightmares of my people became my own along with their fears, anxieties and nocturnal horrors."

Bank captures, exquisitely, the mood of the camp that undulates between periods of intense creativity and productivity on the one hand and yet profound sorrow and desolation on the other. Cold, frightening, factual statistics are comingled with rich, subjective, expressive descriptions of impressive human talent and ability. Terezin is fully cognizant of the fact that it's very existence is "...nothing but a charade – a sham...a sinister specter stoking their worst fears..." Nothing can fully prepare the reader for the inevitable devastation that lies ahead other than heartfelt expressions of pride in the extraordinary heroism of ordinary people, temporary though it may be.

This loving "memoir" is dedicated to the memory of Bank's grandparents, Ludwig and Sophie Frank who, despite all odds, survived their interment at Terezin. In the end, all that's left of the camp is the eternal veil of memory that can never be erased. "I am nothing more than memory; and it is memory of which I am composed and it is memory through which I can be reached...So long as there is a memory of me...I am alive." As such, each of us is implored to be Terezin's "Kaddishel;" the one who will faithfully recite the mourner's prayer for a place that so desperately tried to offer comfort and consolation but, instead, thanks to its merciless overlords, only exacted retribution and revenge.

I Am Terezin is essential reading for anyone interested in the Nazi Holocaust. In so many respects it defies description and yet it's mercurial story must be told so that we never forget man's grotesque inhumanity to man. Out of the tear-soaked pages of this book lies a world still waiting to be redeemed...

Rabbi Robert S. Leib

Old York Road Temple-Beth Am, Abington, PA

Acknowledgments

The first completed draft of my book about Theresienstadt was traditional nonfiction. The second completed draft was written more creatively as narrative nonfiction probably because I had begun teaching creative nonfiction in an MFA program. But something was missing and I was struck with the idea to tell the camp's story as a "memoir" in the voice of the camp; but the voice was elusive and likely would have remained so without the invaluable aid of Ari Bank who helped bring the voice to life.

I knew that finding a publisher who would appreciate this unorthodox approach would be daunting and I was most fortunate in having Joe Lerro acquire the manuscript and then with keen insight edit it for content. Although written in the style of fiction, my book must be a true account and aiding in this regard was Alexa Flood who not only acted as copy editor but also provided thorough fact checking. I thought that the cover of my last book, Feig, would never be surpassed and yet Sarah Eldridge who designed the Feig cover, did just that in capturing the very essence of I Am Terezin. In putting everything in place to produce a coherent work for the reader, I could not have asked for a more professional and understanding person than Eric McDermott. My gratitude to Dr. Shrikrishna (Krish) Singh, the publisher of Auctus, whose passion is to provide a vehicle for authors to reach readers with books of value not likely to be considered by typical commercial publishers.

And a special thanks to Hayden Bank, great-great-grandson of Ludwig and Sophie Frank, for the photography utilized on the cover and at such a young age taking to heart the importance of keeping memory alive.

PREFACE

Ich bin Theresienstadt. In order to understand who I am or, perhaps more precisely, what I am, one must begin with my name. Theresienstadt is a German word and my preferred name. After all, wasn't I conceived by Germans on German soil? Was not the purpose of my life set in motion in the serene Berlin suburb of Wannsee? Wasn't I spoken of in the language of Goethe and Schiller as I evolved from an ethereal concept into a living entity breathing life and death into the stones and mortar composing my body?

But as the years following my demise passed, it became popular to refer to me in the Czechoslovakian vernacular by calling me *Terezín*. I suppose this is understandable given the harsh, guttural resonance of the language of my progenitors and the way the final syllable of my name leaves the chin clenched and the tongue flicking the teeth, while on the other hand, my Czech name affects relaxed lips with the *n* floating off endlessly into nowhere. Can I blame people for preferring something other than my original name as I am consigned to the ages? And especially when it is a sound more pleasing to the senses and less jarring on the memory?

While I often oblige by referring to myself in the Czech, my name does, indeed, reveal a good deal about me. For one thing, like me, there has never been anything consistent about my name—an appellation referring to the city built northwest of Prague in 1780 by Emperor Joseph II, which he constructed as a fortress to protect Prague from attacks emanating from the North. Ever the dutiful son, Joseph II christened this village in honor of his mother, Maria Teresia. The Czechs called the town Terezín.

A little more than a century and a half later, the Nazi huns swept over the Czech border, and the garrison- town found itself under the jurisdiction of the Third Reich. The Germans called the town Theresienstadt, the name by which I would generally be referred to in early Holocaust literature. But soon, other names were adopted that bore more subtle and sinister connotations. Once the Nazis decided to use the city for the purpose of furthering their goal of making the world Judenfrei (free of Jews), the town was called Theresienbad, meaning Spa Theresien, and the Jews, mainly the German Jews, were informed they were simply being relocated to a wonderful place where they could indulge themselves in mineral baths.

After a while, this ruse became too outlandish even for the cynical Nazis, and the city took on the designation Judische Selbstverwaltung, translating as Jewish Self-Administration, reflecting the illusion that the city was run by a Jewish administrative body. Later, when the camp was designated as a relocation center for German Jews over the age of sixty, it was sometimes referred to as Reichsaltersheim, or State of Old People's Home.

But enough of this. So much confusion over a name! What matters is my essence, my nature, what makes me who I am. And of even greater importance: what it is that qualifies me to tell the story that follows.

To comprehend my composition, you must suspend your belief that the world is as it seems. You must try to think past the three dimensions and consider the possibility—no, make that the probability—that there is more to reality than you can see, feel, and understand. For I am *sui generis;* just as the Holocaust stands alone among the atrocities humans have perpetrated upon other humans, I stand alone in the midst of the madness that engulfed the Holocaust.

I am *Terezín*. I repeat that in the most existential way: I am *Terezín*. I am the repository of all the souls who touched me from the moment of my conception until the last Jew trudged out from under my gray portico without even a backward glance over the shoulder nor a word of good-bye, leaving me out of sight and, I hope, out of mind. I am the synthesis of innocence and evil, of victims and perpetrators, of peoples of many nationalities speaking in diverse tongues, of collaborators willing and unwilling, of people choosing to see what they want to see, sometimes to deceive themselves and sometimes to deceive others. I am a compilation of ambiguity, and if it is clarity you seek, you will not find it in me.

Like all memoirs, mine is a story but not of the standard fare because, if for no other reason, it is not recounted in a solitary voice. Rather, my narrative spills from the quivering lips and compressed jaws of a unified, collective cadence composed of all those Jews who lived within me during the brief period I existed and for whatever amount of time—days, months, or years—they were compelled to call me their home. As for their number, although each and every person is a part of me, the exact figure has proven elusive. It has been calculated by some to a precise integer but not always consistent; one statistician recounts 141,162, while another reports 139,654, and yet others wisely and cautiously suggest approximately 139,000 or 140,000 or 141,000. That we have any numbers at all is only because of the fastidiousness of the Germans and their penchant for meticulous record keeping. With this thought in mind, I prefer to keep the numbers round.

Now you may ask, why, given the thousands of accounts written about the Holocaust, should my story be told? What can be learned from my existence that doesn't pale in comparison to the fiery flames that consumed the corpses in the ovens of the death camps? Or the ricocheting bullets in the killing pits? Or the wailing babies torn from their mothers' arms, hurled in the air, and shot on descent? You will find none of this in my life which, I submit, is precisely the point.

Evil has many faces, and it is often the most insidious that should be feared above all others and few of which, I suggest, have ever been more guileful than the mask embedded on my visage. And because it is so easy to dismiss me and toss me aside, to forget me and neatly file me away amongst the evils perpetrated in the Holocaust, is precisely the reason why the lesson to be learned from my existence is singular and most instructive.

Indeed, not even I knew who I was in the beginning. In the earliest days of my existence, I believed what was said about me, and I eagerly looked forward to establishing myself as a Jewish city run by Jews accountable to no one but themselves. Where on earth has there ever been such a place in the last 2,000 years until the establishment of the modern State of Israel! Can you blame me for being excited at such a prospect?

Although I was forced to concede that the concept of functioning as an independent Jewish municipality had proven illusory by the time the first transport from

Germany had arrived excreting its cargo of old Jews, I still believed there was a noble purpose to be served as a home for the aged. I would become a spa for the elderly, just as the Germans had promised and in spite of the harsh environs! But soon, too, this delusion fell by the wayside as lists of names were compiled to fill transports hurling thousands of my residents to the East and to an unknown fate which all too soon became evident to even the most optimistic and credulous among them.

So if I could be fooled into not knowing what I had become, then could it have been much of a surprise that the rest of the world was equally deceived? Perhaps this is why, in the earliest decades following my passing, it seemed I was destined to be lost to the ages. Very little was written about me, and what was written was eclipsed by camps like Auschwitz, Treblinka, and Bergen-Belsen. In fact, the fabrication created about my life remained unquestioned—that I had been the best of all possible venues where Jews were confined in Nazi-occupied Europe and not such a bad place to live out the War.

The tragedy is that like the Red Cross delegation who allowed themselves to be duped into believing the façade of Hitler's charade, I continued to be regarded as the preeminent of Europe's depositories for Jews during the Holocaust. Even as more became known about me with memoirs penned, books written, and films made, especially those about the artists and musicians, the veneer remained impenetrable, interning the truth secreted behind the shadowy bulwarks of my walls.

But like slugs slogging through the mud, slowly the facts emerged. People began to discover that the concentration camp Theresienstadt was an awful and terrible place to be, a surrealistic world riddled with fear and deception, disease and death. What is more, there was something singular about me that differentiated me from any of the ghettos, concentration camps, killing camps, and labor camps that Hitler's Holocaust spawned.

Ironically, the one designation that brought me to the world's attention more than any other was when I became known as the Paradise Ghetto, a label the Nazis assiduously avoided when referring to me. Not that the Nazis objected to the delusion that I was a paradise of sorts, a notion they asked the world to accept as proof that Hitler was good to his Jews. But they did object to the word ghetto, which they strove to evade.

Oddly enough, the Nazis had a valid point in this regard. There is a good argument to be made that I was not a ghetto but not for the reasons the Nazis would have had the world believe. Ghetto is too generous a term for what truly took place within my walls which brings us to the conundrum of assigning me to a proper classification. Was I a concentration camp? A ghetto? A transit camp? A death camp? Or something entirely unique for which all appellations fail?

However, one thing is clear: once the local Czechs were ordered to vacate the fortress-town, my only residents were Jews. Interestingly, this in itself makes me one of a kind in the camps of the Shoah, because I was the only camp set aside exclusively for Jews—no communists, no POWs, no gypsies, no homosexuals, no political dissidents—only Jews had the privilege of becoming my official denizens during the span of my life. Even the priests who conducted Christmas Mass in 1943 possessed sufficient Jewish blood coursing through their veins to qualify as Jewish according to the Nazi racial laws.

So, back to the question: Was I a ghetto? In Jewish history, the marginalization of Jews in Christian Europe took on a physical component with Jewish sectors demarcated as early as the eleventh century. In 1492, the Jews of Krakow in Poland were ordered to live within specific, walled sections of the city.

However, it was in 1509 that ghettos became firmly entrenched in Christian Europe when a group of Jewish immigrants, ironically hailing from Germany, were granted permission to take up residence in Venice provided they lived on a small island located among the city's canals and enclosed by a high wall. This quarter was known as the *Ghetto Nuovo*, or New Foundry, because it was where metal was smelted for making canons, and such places were called *geto* in Venetian dialect.

Soon, the practice caught on in other cities. In 1555, the Pope decreed that Jews be compelled to live in a swampy area on the left bank of the Tiber River. This ghetto would be separated from the rest of Rome by an enclosed wall. Throughout the remaining part of the century, other Italian states adopted similar ghettos for their Jews.

Generally, during the day, Jews were free to leave the ghetto for work and other activities, but at night, they were obliged to return and stay put to avoid intermingling with their Christian neighbors. In this respect, I was a ghetto, although in the extreme sense, because like other ghettos established by the German's during the War, the Jews were confined both day and night. But what made me so ideally suited as a ghetto was my physical appearance as a fortress-town.

Throughout the centuries in Western Europe, almost all ghettos shared the physical properties of being demarcated by a moat, hedge, or some sort of bulwark and as you will see, I had it all. Yet, what transpired within my city-fortress walls took me well beyond what is commonly referred to as a ghetto, since the Nazis had more sinister designs in store for my inhabitants than mere confinement and segregation.

Nor do I neatly fit into any of the categories of the camps established by the Third Reich. I was not conceived to execute the mass murder of my inmates as were Bełżec, Sobibór, Treblinka, Majdanek, and Auschwitz, although some of these camps served the dual function of a labor camp. Neither was I merely a transit camp, since more than a third of my residents lived out the remainder of their lives within me or were liberated upon my demise. And while my inhabitants were compelled to perform labor, for the most part, the work was to provide the needed resources for their survival.

By the process of elimination, although labor was demanded and people died by the thousands, it seems I come closest to resembling a concentration camp, or *Konzentrationslager*, like Dachau, Sachsenhausen, Buchenwald, Mauthausen, and Ravensbrück. Such camps comprised an area under the exclusive control of the *Schutzstaffel* (SS) and were originally established to terrorize the population as a place where dissidents and undesirables were dispatched into a dark cavernous hole from which most never emerged.

Nonetheless, I remained unique even among the concentration camps. As I have said, from my inception, I was designed exclusively for Jews. Moreover, the SS exerted its control circuitously and more cunningly like a puppeteer pulling the strings from somewhere beyond the shadowy clouds that hung above my parapets, leaving it to the Jewish administration to implement their orders.

In any event, I have settled upon calling myself a concentration camp because, if for no other reason, the Jews who lived in my domain were reminded of it every waking hour as they wore the mandatory white and red armbands which bore their respective names: last name first, with letters running through the center in bold print reading *K. L. Terezín;* the *K* and the *L* stood for *Konzentrationslager*, the SS's own admission that Theresienstadt was anything but a Jewish city or ghetto. And to bolster my decision to refer to myself as a concentration camp are the official-looking documents resembling passports issued after the War by the Displaced Person (D.P.) Center in Deggendorf that were embossed with the photos of those who survived, confirming the dates of their duration in "the concentration camp *Terezín*."

• • •

Because I am a quite organized and efficient entity, my life story will be told in a mostly linear way beginning with the beginning and concluding with the end of my terrestrial days. In Chapter One, you will see the place where I was conceived— ironically, a beautiful, tranquil milieu in the Berlin suburb of Wannsee where the Third Reich had established a recreation center for the SS to take in the luscious foliage and serene waters of the emerald lake. Nestled along the banks of Lake Wannsee and given the seclusion and intimacy the setting provided, SS Obergruppenführer Reinhard Heydrich believed he had found the perfect place to establish the protocol for what would become the Final Solution of the Jewish question.

On January 20, 1942, a meeting was convened by Heydrich and his assistant, Adolf Eichmann, with delegates from all the pertinent authorities needed to coordinate the resources required to rid the world of the Jews. Those present did not mince words about killing Jews and the various methods to implement the plan. But in order to effi- ciently and effectively murder millions of people, it soon became clear that the victims would have to be gathered together prior to their actual execution. Thus, the decision was made that the Jews in all occupied territories as well as the Jews of Germany would be collected in temporary ghettos from where they would be moved to the East for the Final Solution.

Only weeks earlier, the city of Theresienstadt had been designated as a ghetto for selected Jews of the Protectorate, Jews from Bohemia and Moravia, the precursor of modern Czechoslovakia, who were my first inhabitants. Although at Heydrich's specific instructions I was to become a ghetto for German Jews over sixty-five or who were decorated veterans of the First World War, it was decided that the camp would serve an additional function. I would be a way station for tens of thousands of Jews destined for the death camps. It was at this moment in time that the nefarious purpose of my life was set in motion.

On November 24, 1941, the first convoy consisting of 342 Jewish men from the Protectorate arrived to make me habitable. On May 9, 1945, the camp Theresien- stadt was liberated by the Russians who discovered 16,832 Jews still alive. In the following pages spanning the 1,263 days that marked the duration of my life as the concentration camp *Terezín,* I hope to share my story and that of the Jews who lived and died within my ramparts.

CHAPTER ONE: I AM CONCEIVED

Names and words are very important to me, not only the ordinary meanings but the subliminal, the innuendos, the concealed truths secreted away behind the vernacular. So naturally, the name of my birthplace is of some consequence. Interestingly, like my own name, the province which I consider my official birthplace has more than one connotation.

To the people of Germany during the first few decades of the twentieth century, the word Wannsee conjured visions of a crystalline lake reflecting a perfectly clear, blue sky and a panorama dotted with white, billowing sails. Moreover, having the Berlin lakeside suburb of Wannsee as a residential address drew the envy of all Germans. But beginning with the second half of the twentieth century, the word was likely to mean other things: a word that most people outside of the area did not recognize; a word that most Germans preferred to forget; and a word that when coupled with conference referred to the time and place where, for all intents and purposes, the mechanism was set into motion for ridding Europe of its eleven million Jews. Less-known is the fact that Wannsee is where I was given birth.

Now, I am not an ordinary being allowed months within the comfort and isolation of the womb to fully develop. There was no bonding with a mother to nurture me; indeed, I have no mother. From the instant I was conceived some weeks before the Wannsee Conference and designated to be a city for the Jews of Nazi-occupied Bohemia and Moravia, I was forced to mature in a harsh and uninviting world. Hence, my official birth date—the day and year I came into my own with my purpose in life fully established—is January 20, 1942, when the Wannsee Conference was held.

Of course, I wanted to know as much as I could about the place of my origin even though I was there for only the shortest amount of time, merely hours, not even a full day. What I learned proved to be ironic, for I was brought forth into this world in an edifice of profound beauty and magnificence that provided a stark contrast to the dilapidated, decomposing environs where I would expire. Far better to have had it the other way around, if for no other reason than one remembers so little of one's birth, but the moments of one's passing remain for an eternity.

Appropriately enough, the villa that housed the Wannsee Conference where I was born was built in the same year as the commencement of World War I, which many believe paved the way for the conditions enabling Hitler and his National Socialist Party to seize control of the German Republic. Ernst Marlier, a wealthy Berlin industrialist with visions of Neoclassical and Greek Revival styles in his mind's eye, commissioned the construction of the three-story brick and mortar building.

The approach to Marlier's villa was a private road with matured trees and sweeping branches evenly set on either side. The road ended at a circular driveway with a perennial garden blooming in the center. Perhaps this is why I always loved gardens, and no matter how dire conditions became for me, particularly in my last year, there was always a plot of earth within my walls where a garden was tended— frequently by the children. But back to Marlier's mansion where everything was designed to impress with its imposing columns, masonry canopy, and thirty-one windows looming over the garden and driveway. Inside the villa, the library and elegant salons left lasting impressions on all visitors and guests. However, this was not to last, and Marlier's affluence was fleeting. Due to Germany's severely depressed economy following World War I, he was forced to sell his beloved villa in 1921 to Friedrich Minoux, another German industrialist but one more fortunate than Marlier. Minoux supported the burgeoning right-wing political movement and aligned himself with Adolf Hitler and the National Socialist Party. In fact, in the 1920s, Minoux's mansion became a regular meeting place for right-wing politicians.

By 1941, the Wannsee villa was owned by the SS-Nordhav Foundation to be used as a guesthouse for SS officials. The mansion provided the perfect edifice and Wannsee the sublime setting for SS Lieutenant General Reinhard Heydrich, Chief of the Security Police and Security Service, to summon the men he would need to implement the Final Solution to the Jewish problem. When I am asked to single out one person as my father, it is always Reinhard Heydrich whom I designate.

Heydrich was not yet thirty-eight when he convened one of the most sinister meetings in history. But in every way, he was the man for the job. Heydrich could have been the embodiment for the Nazi Party. Unlike Hitler and his inner circle, Heydrich's physical appearance was the image of the true Aryan. He was blond, handsome, and towered over those hovering around him. His hair was perfectly parted just off-center above an unusually high and prominent forehead.

Yet, if one took the time to study him further as I had, to go past the first impressions his presence commanded, one could see the imperfections in his countenance. His eyes were a shade too small for the seamless, oblong face, and they shifted restlessly from here to there. His hands were too slender for one so tall and resembled the spindly legs of a spider. When he spoke, instead of the bold and booming voice one expected from such a bearing, his speech was delivered in much too high a pitch, and the words burst out like bullets in a nervous staccato. And finally, his otherwise splendid figure was marred by wide hips, so when he walked, he walked like a woman.

What endeared Heydrich to Hitler and Heinrich Himmler, head of the SS, was the confidence and ruthlessness with which he conducted himself. His superiors felt he was a natural given his history as a gifted athlete, champion skier, and fearless pilot. Heydrich held no court for either friend or foe who stood in his way or who failed to carry out his orders to his satisfaction. So feared was he that he would be known in occupied Europe as The Hangman, and among his colleagues, Heydrich, the friendless loner, was more dreaded than respected.

The fate of SS Lieutenant General Heydrich and the Jews of Czechoslovakia was bound together when Hitler appointed Heydrich as Protector of Bohemia and Moravia. The people living in this conquered territory that became known as the Protectorate during Nazi occupation fell under the rule of Reinhard Heydrich. One of Heydrich's first proclamations was a promise to rid the land of its Jews. Although Heydrich set the mechanism in motion to achieve this end, he did not live to see the results. On May 27, 1942, while driving from his residence to his office in Prague in an open Mercedes, daring the rumored assassins to take their best shot, two young Czechs dispatched from London obliged him by tossing a grenade that exploded fragments into his spleen, inflicting wounds from which he succumbed a week later.

Heydrich relished the power he wielded and wanted no ambiguities regarding what was to be the Final Solution to the Jewish Problem. He sought to make it perfectly clear that Final Solution no longer meant voluntary emigration, confinement in ghettos, or removal to concentration camps. Final Solution would mean one thing only—the extermination of the Jewish race.

Toward this end, he convened the infamous Conference on January 20, 1942 at the SS-owned villa in Wannsee. In addition to himself and his assistant, SS Lieutenant Colonel Adolf Eichmann, thirteen men were present, representing the government and military branches needed to implement the Final Solution. Heydrich was meticulous in every way, and despite the gruesome nature of the subject, minutes were recorded, which he personally edited before the final protocol was transcribed for posterity. Years later, the world also learned what transpired from oral testimony, particularly that of Adolf Eichmann, the man most responsible for executing the Final Solution.

Not wishing to put up with time consuming-questions or debate, Heydrich lulled his guests into a sense of complacency as they stuffed themselves with a mid-day buffet luncheon. The SS Lieutenant General then effortlessly took charge of the meeting, beginning with a brief history of the Nazi endeavors to resolve the Jewish Problem. But more is required, he emphasized, squaring off his shoulders and looming over the table, in order to ensure that in the end, there will be no Jews left to "form the germ cell of a new Jewish revival." Heydrich halted and took a moment, scanning all eyes in the room to make certain his co-conspirators comprehended the full nature of what he implied: There would be no chance for the vermin race to propagate and create a future, no offspring to wreak revenge. It was at that moment that the fate of the children who would enter my domain was sealed.

The Conference lasted less than an hour and a half, and by the time it came to a close, Heydrich had established his supremacy over the official apparatus that was to deal with Europe's eleven million Jews. But in the plan of operations for transports and way stations, concentration camps, labor camps, and death camps, a tiny niche was carved out by Heydrich himself.

Every Jew—man, woman, and child—will be dealt with in the same fashion, Heydrich declared. The nods and subtle smiles of the men around the table knew what Heydrich meant by dealt with. However, an exception is required, he continued, for German and Austrian Jews who meet one of three prerequisites: being over the age of sixty-five (later lowered to sixty); disabled or highly decorated WWI veterans; or persons of sufficient celebrity who would generate domestic or foreign inquiry. Those Jews who fulfilled the third requirement would come to be referred to by my other denizens as the prominents.

Indeed, Heydrich went on, it was only yesterday that Eichmann visited the town that will serve as the shop window to the world proving how well the Third Reich treats its old Jews. It is a small town, just outside Prague and only an hour or two's walk from the train station located in a village called Bauschowitz. Giving a nod in Eichmann's direction, Heydrich announced that his estimable assistant will manage this settlement. The name of the town? Theresienstadt, Heydrich replied with a smile, as if proclaiming the name of his newborn child. And so I was born.

The town Heydrich singled out for this devious purpose was built in 1780 by Joseph II, Emperor of Austria-Hungary, to protect the main road from Prussia to Prague against the attacks of Frederick II of Prussia, though no combat then or for the next 160 years even came close to its parapets. Joseph II named the town after his mother, Maria Theresa, who was remembered by Jews for ordering the mass expulsions of 1744-1748. Although autocratic in his rule, Joseph II was more disposing toward the Jews and allowed them a certain degree of freedom.

At the same time Theresienstadt was constructed, an old fort was built at the other end of the stone bridge that crossed the Eger River, a river that ran slow and calm during most of the year at the foot of the town. This small fort had been used by the Austrian government to incarcerate both common and political criminals, but during the time of my reign, the small fort became known as the Little Fortress, a place that terrified my inhabitants because few who entered were ever seen again.

During the years prior to my coming into being, about 6,000 residents lived within the town's walls, in addition to an equal number of soldiers whose needs the civilians fulfilled by trade and providing refreshment at numerous bars. Ironically, the commander of the garrison, Field Marshal Lieutenant Moritz Edler von Steinsberg, was a Jew.

The act of my conception came about several weeks before my birth when my paterfamilias needed some way to lure the Jews of the Protectorate into believing they would not be hurtled onto transports heading east where they would be pressed into forced labor or murdered. In me, Heydrich found what seemed to be the perfect answer. Officially, as far as these Czech Jews would be told, I was to be a self-sustaining Jewish city and not, as he and Eichmann had decided, the site to temporarily concentrate the Protectorate's Jews before transporting them to the labor and killing camps.

But how was I to be prepared for this task? Eichmann and Heydrich huddled after Eichmann returned from a visit to the town. Because the fortress walls permitted an inner city only 500 to 700 meters square, Eichmann had to admit the town was small. But on the other hand, there were advantages. Pushing back black-frame glasses over the bridge of his nose as he was wont to do, Eichmann pointed out the benefits: the barracks could easily provide mass residences; no substantial guard force was required; and best of all, the towering fortification would serve the dual function of keeping those within the walls from escaping as well as keeping outsiders from learning what was going on inside.

So it was decided. The leadership of the Jewish population in the Protectorate would be informed of the location of their very own Jewish city to be administered by a Council of Elders comprised of Jews under the supervision of the German authority. Two lists of candidates were submitted to the Germans by the Jewish community from which the German authority would select one. Heading the list chosen by the Germans was Jakob Edelstein, the man who would be responsible for creating this unique Jewish city and overseeing its day-to-day operations. In time, Edelstein would become known as the Elder of the Jews.

At first, I thought Edelstein lacked sufficient experience for the job. After all, at thirty-eight, he certainly was no elder, although he was the same age as Heydrich. And with his Semitic dark, wavy hair, fleshy face, and bleak eyes peering from black, round spectacles, what a contrast he bore to my paterfamilias! For a time, these two men were the most important people in my life, and yet, they could not have been more different.

As a Zionist, Edelstein proved dedicated to the task and was excited about establishing a self-sustaining Jewish city which could serve as a prototype for re-settling Jews in Palestine where his people could attain a degree of independence. Edelstein's enthusiasm was infectious, and I came to share it—at least in my earliest days. As a result, an aura pervaded the air, instilling those inside me with the feeling that despite the hopelessness facing them, I could be a beacon to a future where one day, Jews could live and flourish independently.

However, Edelstein had his reservations whether Heydrich had made the correct choice in the location. Edelstein was familiar with *Terezín* from his days as a traveling salesman, and with a mere 219 buildings, he could not visualize 50,000 Jews settled there. Edelstein dispatched a representative to have a more thorough look.

The report brought back was bleak. Edelstein furrowed his forehead, pondering the pages. The level of underground water running beneath the fortress was high, and behind the stone walls were subterranean cellars. Everything must be damp, Edelstein frowned. Most of the living quarters had not been used in twenty years and are likely unhabitable. The town is one giant health hazard, Edelstein diplomatically suggested to the Nazis.

But Edelstein's reservations fell on deaf ears. On October 10, 1941, Heydrich and Eichmann made up their minds. By the end of the month, I was the officially designated city for the Protectorate's Jewish population. A thirty-year-old Austrian Nazi Party member, Siegfried Seidl, who had made a name for himself transporting Jews to Poland, was appointed the commandant.

Jakob Edelstein accepted the German decision with ambivalence. Folding his arms on his desk and leaning forward, he parted his lips, revealing enough teeth so that if someone observing didn't know better, it looked almost as though he were smiling. On the one hand, Edelstein ruminated, he would rather continue his efforts arranging for Jews to immigrate to Palestine where their presence was sorely needed. After all, that is why he had repeatedly refused opportunities for himself, his wife, and young son to make the voyage to the future Jewish homeland. I always admired Edelstein for this selfless dedication, which ultimately demanded that he and his loved ones pay the final price. Yet on the other hand, he admitted to himself, here is an opportunity to prove that Jews could govern themselves and be self-sufficient, which would be invaluable in convincing the world of the legitimacy of a Jewish state in Palestine once the Germans were defeated and sanity was restored.

But in the end, he had no real choice in the matter. This decision, like so many decisions he would later appear to make, was not really his own. Sighing and leaning back in his chair, Edelstein resolved to take up the challenge and make *Terezín* a model city where Jews could live until able to return to their homes in Bohemia and Moravia or move to Palestine once the Third Reich was brought to its knees.

And so, on December 4, 1941, Jakob Edelstein and his colleagues, mostly friends from the Zionist youth movement, boarded the train to Theresienstadt to establish the Jewish administration of the Jewish town. Upon their arrival, no special attention was paid by the German guards at the station nor the Czech civilians to this band of men carrying small suitcases at their sides. Conversing and sometimes even joking amongst themselves as they bounded from the train, the only concern on their minds was whether they could find their way without getting lost trekking from the train station to *Terezín*.

Because the Jewish delegation made one wrong turn after another, the two-mile walk from the Bauschowitz station took much longer than the hour or so it should have. The congenial conversations transformed into griping and complaining until finally, a somber silence descended upon the slowly moving group. Arms ached as the suitcases they lugged grew heavier and heavier. Edelstein was not the only one to grow concerned that this hike would make a poor first impression upon the Jewish arrivals who will follow in their footsteps.

Finally, after asking for directions and being told to keep their sight set on *Terezín's* church steeple that loomed on the horizon, the entourage arrived at their destination. With hesitant steps, they crossed the drawbridge that spanned a deep moat. Edelstein dropped his suitcase, set his hands on his hips, and took a deep breath. The men around him did likewise, lifting their eyes at what rose before them: a town like no other they had ever seen.

At first glance, *Terezín* did not appear threatening at all. In fact, since the roofs of the complicated defense installations were all dirt-covered, allowing for the growth of luxuriant lawns and stands of trees, the scene was inviting. But at further inspection, Edelstein and his companions understood why this site was chosen.

The men cowered below brick walls approximately fifty to sixty feet in height and several yards thick that ran in a zigzag line. Past this barrier lay moats twenty to thirty yards wide that combined with thick shrubbery to create a dampness that would permeate every article of clothing, fabric, surface of skin, and parcel of food, and settle into the nostrils, lungs, and bones of anyone living within the fortification. This dankness would remain a constant companion to every Jew who resided behind the brick walls.

Edelstein stood with his companions at one of Theresienstadt's two entrances. In all other respects, the town was sealed off from the rest of the world by its ramparts and moats. Beyond the moats arose another brick wall with barred windows and arched gateways, which were the entrances to the casements that once housed soldiers. The

Jewish delegation could not see from their vantage point how the walls, moats, and fortifications formed a double ring around the town. But had they been birds, able to fly and soar above, they would have perceived how Theresienstadt appeared as an eight-pointed star. Inside the walls and moats, the town itself was laid out in military precision with five streets lengthwise and twelve cross streets filled with square blocks of houses. The large streets were indicated by the letter L while the cross streets with a Q followed by the house number.

The center of the town consisted of a large public square. There were two wide-ranging parks and two smaller parks. Taking their first tentative steps into *Terezín*, Edelstein and his companions were struck by the grotesque shapes of the bare trees that in the spring filled with foliage but in winter looked more like distorted skeletons. In the midst of the trees, there was a sandy parade ground.

Making their way along the symmetrically aligned sidewalks, the group passed the abandoned church and schools, the corner tower, and the empty City Hall, constructed in an overly ornate style with the roof having two slopes on each of its four sides. The City Hall would become the dreaded SS headquarters. Although 3,500 townspeople were still residing in Theresienstadt, and would for another six months until only the Jews and their guards remained, most of the houses and businesses were shuttered and empty. There were no people to be seen. Not a sound was heard.

Looking around, Edelstein and his men were crestfallen. Why were things so desolate? Where was the housing for the thousands of Jews who were scheduled to follow in only a matter of days? The barracks they passed tramping through *Terezín's* streets were shoddy. The odor of rot was everywhere. What of the 342 men Edelstein had dispatched ten days earlier; what have they been doing all this time? Certainly not making the proper preparations! Edelstein fumed.

Finally, the delegation came upon a barracks that appeared at least livable with activity going on inside. There was electricity. Lights flickered behind the bare windows. The men entered to be greeted with upturned, apathetic faces, many with grime on their foreheads. No smiles or words of encouragement. Rows of squinting, bleak eyes burned with resentment, bitterness, and anger arising from their sense of frustration in not having sufficient supplies to fulfill their assigned task. Mouths were shut and lips drawn tight for fear of saying something that couldn't be taken back.

After a prolonged moment with silence hanging in the air like a leaden balloon, one of the men slowly lifted himself from where he sat. He shuffled over to

Edelstein while the new arrivals, one by one, were beginning to drop their suitcases on the barracks's dusty floor. Reaching Edelstein, who was well-known to many of the Jews of the Protectorate and whose face would be imprinted on the ghetto's currency, the man stopped not more than a foot from the official who had delegated to him and his company the task of preparing the ghetto. His lips twisted into a wry grin as he spewed his few words of welcome: "And now, gentlemen, you're in shit."

Edelstein and his companions settled into a room on the first floor of the wide-arched Sudeten barracks. Later, they would be transferred to the more desirable Magdeburg barracks. Lacking an office, Edelstein worked out of his suitcase to make preparations for 8,000 Jews scheduled to arrive in the next several days. Despite Heydrich's promise that no Jews would be sent to Theresienstadt until proper living quarters had been established and basic conditions met, the first transport of Jews arrived the very next day into a world of mayhem and havoc.

I had hoped to provide a more hospitable environment for my denizens, but nothing went as expected. The weather was dismal, dreary, gray, and bleak when the first transport of 1,000 Jews, whose original destination had been Minsk, was diverted my way. Instead of cattle cars, transports from Prague made use of ordinary passenger trains, but nonetheless, the two-day journey was no pleasure because despite the fact that each transport was numbered, and everyone had their own seats, the conditions were overcrowded and unsanitary. And then there was the matter of nourishment. People had to subsist on whatever food and drink they had brought along, and it was never enough to last. But there was the opportunity to take in the beautiful Bohemian landscape with blooming fields, trees, and cattle slowly masticating grass. In this way, the travelers were not alarmed nor their suspicions aroused for what truly lay ahead.

Once the train pulled into the Baushowitz station, the passengers alighted and gathered up their belongings. For some, this meant scurrying onto the tracks where the baggage had tumbled in the chaos of debarking with people bumbling about while the train pulled out. Luggage in hand, everyone lined up four and five abreast, waiting for the trek to their new home to begin. Slowly the throng moved along, passing the two-story gray-stoned buildings with sloping shingled roofs on their left.

Each new arrival was required to present an inventory of all valuables left behind, making it an easy task for the Nazis to confiscate them later. Indeed, the magnitude of what was appropriated from these Czech Jews was staggering by any standard. The Nazis looted and shipped to Germany some 778,000 books, 603 pianos, 21,000 carpets, and whatever else they deemed worth the effort.

As for what the Jews were permitted to bring along, most of this was also commandeered. In a procedure referred to as the *schleusen*, the contents of the luggage were sorted. The newcomers were warned by the SS not to hide money or jewelry and to surrender any such valuables. Though almost everyone complied, just to make certain, body checks were conducted with the females examined by particularly repulsive-looking German women recruited from nearby Leitmeritz. These women were derisively called *beroshky*, meaning beetles in ghetto language. The luggage was inspected by Czech gendarmes, three-fourths of which was systematically pilfered. What little remained, if anything, was returned to the rightful owner. By that summer, the Germans had streamlined the procedure and simply confiscated everything other than the hand luggage, which was still examined and mostly disappeared.

The clouds hung heavy in the soggy air when the thousand Jews from the first transport plodded in my direction. Because of the thick mist that arose from the moats, they could not see me until they were almost upon the foot of my fortress walls. At first a state of confusion prevailed as the arrivals filled my streets, and no one knew where to go. But then the Germans took over, ordering men housed in barracks separate from women and children. This meant that families were driven apart. Young men and women would not be able to court, wed, and build families. There was no future for the Jews of *Terezín*.

The pretense that I was a relatively decent place to live and, to some extent, provide a resemblance to the lives my inhabitants had previously led was shattered to bits and pieces just as effectively as a sledgehammer smashing a rock to smithereens. There was only a hellish present replacing a past that grew more distant and illusory with each passing day.

Trying to explain to the increasingly belligerent complaints of his constituency that he was not to blame for this situation, Edelstein quickly recognized that in the single command, breaking up families, issued by the Germans, a pattern had been established. Like a master puppeteer, the Germans controlled the Jewish marionettes who supposedly were in charge of those residing within my fortress walls. Shoulders sagging, Edelstein's face exposed the sadness he felt in acknowledging that *Terezín* was not to be the independent, self-sustaining Jewish city he had dreamed of but rather just one more labor camp where the Jews would be confined and sent to work—perhaps even to their deaths.

Nonetheless, much remained to be completed if I were to be ready to receive the expected throngs. Edelstein and the other officials made preparations for the ten existing barracks to become habitable. But it soon became apparent that the over-crowding conditions, which began almost immediately, would make this impossible. In most rooms, twenty to forty beds were pushed against each other, leaving only a central aisle to move around. One's bed became the only place where one could be alone, yet even this was not entirely true since there were often unwanted bedmates. Pandemics of bedbugs were frequent, and the merciless parasites attacked every part of the body with their painful stings. People were driven from their beds carting pillows, covers, sheets, cushions, anything that could be used to construct a makeshift bed elsewhere, assuming a space could be secured in the hallways or outside in courtyards, in the attic or on the roof.

Wanting to give some sense of security to the children, Edelstein selected twenty-five-year-old Gonda Redlich to be in charge of their activities and education. Edelstein knew he could count on Gonda whose dedication was beyond question. Instead of leaving for Palestine when he had the opportunity just before the Nazis arrived in Prague, Gonda chose to remain and help others make *aliyah*. Prior to that, he had interrupted his studies as a law student to become a vice principal at a Zionist youth school, which made him perfectly suited for the task assigned to him by Edelstein. What most endeared me to Gonda was that, like me, he was a being with contradictions: despite a delicate body, he possessed great physical strength; his cool, penetrating stare was offset by a warm, forthcoming handshake; and his shy character belied a sharp wit.

After his arrival, Gonda took Gerta Beck for a wife, though it was a marriage that could not be formalized in the traditional sense given the lack of legal recognition I could bestow. From this union, they had a son named Daniel. How ironic, I had thought at the time, that their son bore the name of the biblical Daniel who had been thrown into the lions' den. But unlike that Daniel, their son born in March of 1944 did not survive. Six months after his birth, he and his parents were stowed on a transport heading east. Yes, despite the obstacles, some children were conceived within me, and I loved them all, each and every one. So it pained me terribly whenever one—like Daniel Redlich—became lost to me.

The Jewish Council knew that regulations had to be established, governing all sorts of conduct, such as dress codes, use of water, and electricity. There was a much-debated prohibition on smoking and even the allowable length of hair. Edelstein was determined decorum be maintained and the populace not descend into chaos and madness—or worse, despair. Edelstein established this tone from which his successors never deviated, and for this I was forever grateful. Despite the worst conditions, at least there remained an air of dignity about me.

The Germans were not without their own rules for the Jews. The camp's first commandant, Dr. Siegfried Seidl, was a stickler for military precision and regulations. In short order, the Jews of *Terezín* learned the German words for Attention, Forward March, and Company Halt. They also were required to salute all Germans, even the German teenagers accoutered in SS uniforms. When in the presence of a German, the women had to bow their heads, and the men had to raise their hats. In his own way, Edelstein adopted a personal policy of passive resistance. Despite the harsh winter weather, I would see him striding along the ghetto's streets with his dark, wavy hair billowing in the wind, hatless, so he would not have to tip a hat in deference to a German. The Germans never caught on to this, though I quickly did, and I chuckled to myself each time he passed a German and weaved a few fingers through the strands of his hair.

In less than two weeks, the Jewish hierarchy was formally instituted by Seidl. As previously established, the ghetto would be governed by a Council of Elders with Jacob Edelstein as its head and Otto Zucker as his assistant. The Jews bristled at the selection of the word elder, which they knew the Germans deliberately selected to reflect the fraudulent, nineteenth-century, anti-Semitic document, *The Protocols of the Elders of Zion.*

Three weeks after Edelstein and his companions arrived, an ironic twist of fate took place. It was my first Christmas; fir trees could be seen through the windows of the remaining Christian population. The scent of baked cakes and cookies wafted through the air. Accustomed to celebrating the holiday, many Czech Jews sang Christmas carols in the barracks, hoping that by the next Christmas they would be home.

But the new year brought reality home in the worst way possible. On January 8, 1942, Seidl ordered that a list be compiled of 2,000 names to fill a transport scheduled to leave the following day for the East. The Jewish leadership was shocked.

Everywhere, Jews were wringing their hands and heaving groans of despair. I myself was taken aback with this dramatic turn of events, as I had believed my destiny was to become a self-sustaining city and home to my residents to live out their lives or, more hopefully, a temporary abode until the Nazis were defeated. Now they were informed in the bluntest way possible the ghetto was neither a home nor even a labor camp but worse—a way station for Jews of the Protectorate to be deported east. Edelstein and the Jewish leadership were forced to acknowledge the grim truth when Seidl delegated to the Council the task of composing the list.

This was no small matter and would be the festering lesion that largely defined me. Like a chronic ailment that could arise without warning and lay one so low that life came to a complete standstill, the order to compile a list brought my world to a halt. Previously in Prague when transports were arranged, the Germans furnished the names of those to depart. But now the task was given to the Jews themselves, which brought a sadistic sense of satisfaction to the Germans who derived pleasure watching the Jews strain with the moral dilemma they confronted and seeing to its implementation. Despite the Council's efforts to avoid the assignment, the order stood. Provide the names by dawn.

All night long, the members of the Council struggled to compose the roster of names. The Council of Elders and their staff had entered a surreal world for which they had no compass and were totally unprepared. Two thousand Jews—one in every four of my residents—were to be identified to board trains that would travel east. But what did east mean? Was it another Jewish city like Theresienstadt? Or, perhaps a labor camp where the young would be better off, because how could the Germans expect a good day's work from someone undernourished? Surely inmates in labor camps would be well fed. At least that is what some of the men hunched over the conference table assumed when suggesting that the young be placed on the list.

While this seemed like a sensible rationale, there were others who argued to the contrary, that the young should remain, and their position appeared just as logical. The children were the future, they posited, and at War's end, after the inevitable German defeat, they would be the ones to go to Palestine and pave the way for a new Jewish homeland. Who knows, a growing majority postulated, what fate awaited those journeying east? Although there had been rumors of mass executions—people shot at the gaping edge of deep pits that served as mass graves, even some ramblings about gassings that seemed truly far-fetched—no one could answer the question because no one could even begin to fathom what horror did, in fact, await the Jews at destination's end.

Edelstein unbuttoned the stiff collar of his shirt and set his tie askew. Others rolled up their sleeves. Formalities were abandoned. Difficult work lay ahead in the pre-dawn hours as the men of the Council huddled over 8,000 names from which 2,000 would be culled.

To begin with, an immediate consensus was reached that the Council and its staff were exempt as were doctors and nurses. After much argument, it was decided that, at least for the present, the young would not be placed on the list, and families would remain in tact. Then came the endless bickering, the wheeling and dealing, the favor for a favor as relatives and friends, friends of relatives, relatives of friends, and friends of friends of those wearily slumped over the table were stricken from the list.

As the sun rose on the horizon on the morning of January 9, 1942, Jakob Edelstein dispatched curriers to advise 2,000 Jews to gather their belongings and prepare for transport east. One thousand on the list were to report immediately. The other thousand were to report on January 15.

Bewildered and frightened, the designated Jews amassed at *Terezín's* archway and slowly commenced the hike across the drawbridge to the road leading to the train station at Bauschowitz. Whether the men, women, and even a few children were shivering from fear or from the frigid, below-zero temperature or from both, I can only surmise. But their heads shook, their shoulders quaked, and their legs trembled as they lumbered along the same road they had traversed only several days earlier with hope and high expectations, which I had looked forward to providing but was unable to deliver.

Where they were going, they did not know; nor did I at the time, though I had a foreboding that it would not be good. At first, they were informed the destination was Riga, but by the time they reached the station with the train's engine bellowing smoke into the gray misty air, the end of the line remained a mystery. Somehow even then, I knew within the marrow of my mortar that they were destined for death, and for almost each and every one of them, this proved to be true.

Later that same day, the face of death presented itself in a more direct and horrifying fashion, making it absolutely clear that death would be a constant in the lives of the Jews of *Terezín*. The final veil that concealed the real world the Jews of Theresienstadt were to inhabit was about to be lifted.

Still recovering from the resonance of a thousand pairs of feet shuffling out of the ghetto in the early dawn hours, Edelstein and Zucker were summoned by Seidl and informed that a number of Jews had been sentenced to die for violating German rules. What were these violations? Edelstein and Zucker wanted to know. Concealing the Jewish star in order to go out among the Czech population; letters smuggled out of the ghetto and posted to relatives back home; accidentally brushing against the arm of an SS soldier; and other mundane infractions that in the Nazi *Weltanshlauung* demanded the ultimate price be paid.

Edelstein and Zucker trudged back to the Magdeburg barracks where their offices were located. The entire Council was gathered. Edelstein explained to the crest-fallen faces surrounding him what had to be done. Double gallows were to be erected in the Aussig moat, and twenty-five coffins had to be constructed. Strong rope must be procured. When? Someone asked. By tomorrow morning. Thus, the Jewish police force, uniformed but unarmed Jews responsible for maintaining order, enforcing rules and regulations, and providing assistance to my denizens, were to provide ten of its men to be present in addition to the entire Council of Elders. Someone had to be persuaded to volunteer as executioner. Finally, a short, broad-shouldered man looking like a hunchback by the name of Ada Fischer agreed to perform the duty since he had once been an assistant to an executioner. His only requirement was that he be provided with a bottle of rum and some chewing tobacco to ease his nerves when he finished.

Early the next morning, an icy chill pervaded the flesh and bones of all those present. An eerie silence filled the air since a curfew had been imposed allowing only those summoned to the gallows' site to leave their quarters. Standing stiffly in his gray uniform, Seidl read the official order that sentenced the eleven men to be hanged for violating the rules of German honor. By contrast, Karl Bergel was more animated and seemed to be enjoying himself.

I never cared for Bergel. Not that I held anything but disgust toward all of the three commandants of *Terezín*, but at least I understood there was a trace of humanity in their souls, however slight. But Bergel was one-dimensional; he was the comman-dant of the fortress-town until Seidl arrived, and it was designated a Jewish city. Before the War, Bergel had been a barber. He was a short, squat man whose proclivity to compensate for what he lacked in height and stature made him the perfect bully to order the Jews around. Unlike Seidl, whose countenance was professional, Bergel's dull, crimson face gave one the impression he was always inebriated, which is how he appeared on the foggy morning of the first executions of *Terezín's* Jews.

The execution was an embarrassment to German precision, although ultimately, the objective was accomplished, and eleven corpses were lifted and plunked into awaiting coffins. One of the condemned was ushered by Bergel to the gallows where Bergel called him a coward. Defiantly denying the insult, the man put the hangman's rope over his own neck, securing it improperly. With his feet flailing beneath his swinging torso, the rope broke, and Ada Fischer asked that in accordance with custom, the man be spared a second hanging. Seidl refused, and the man was hung a second time. While inspecting the bodies after all the hangings were carried out, the medical doctor noticed one man was not dead, and he was shot.

The ten Jewish policemen, Dr. Munk, Ada Fischer, Edelstein, Zucker, and the members of the Council of Elders, their bodies aching from the cold and their souls traumatized by the sight of what they were forced to witness, dragged themselves back to the barracks to carry out Seidl's final instruction that the inmates be informed the executions had been carried out. Wanting to avoid further arrests and executions, Edelstein pleaded with everyone to obey the German orders to the letter.

As the sun was making its ascent over my eastern wall, the reality of the Jews' circumstances was brought home. Outside the barricades, the Germans would deceive the world into believing that I was Hitler's gift to the Jews—a self-sustaining city where children played, women sang songs as they carried hoes to the gardens, and the older Jews of the Reich lived out the rest of their lives in tranquility. But within the stone ramparts of the fortress-town, despite their desire to believe the lie and hope for a better future, the 139,654 Jews who tramped under my archway would learn the awful truth: one way or another, almost all of them would be more lives fated for Hitler's Final Solution.

CHAPTER TWO: *ARBEIT MACHT FREI*

One of the more enduring symbols from my time is the iron sign reading *Arbeit Macht Frei* that greeted tens of thousands of my residents when they arrived at my more infamous relation Auschwitz. Less known is that a similar sign formed the top of an archway in my dominion leading to a gate outside the Little Fortress. But truth be known, nowhere in Hitler's hellish realm was the phrase Work Makes Freedom more appropriate than in my domain.

Not that labor resulted in freedom because such a concept eluded Europe's Jews; but it did provide a freedom of sorts—a freedom to try and mitigate the pangs of hunger, the harshness of the elements, and the despondency that life had become. What little my residents possessed they attained as a result of hard work. In this sense, I did, in a sardonic way, bolster Heydrich's contention that I was a self-sustaining city for the Jews because, if the Jews did not work to sustain themselves, each and every last one of them would have been dead within days from arrival.

During my existence, most of the time I was like a beehive buzzing with activity, with scarcely enough space for a person to turn around without bumping into a fellow inmate. An unintended elbow into the back; the heel of a foot stomping on toes; arms flailing about amid thousands scurrying in the streets, cramming in the hallways, sidling in the back alleys. Yet at other times, especially during my last year, I was desolate; my streets were empty, and with most of the young having been dispatched to the East, the elderly slogged along the sidewalks, creeping in silence as though promenading in a funeral procession, which, in a sense, they were. But that was near the end.

During most of my existence, people bustled about everywhere though often with no particular place to go.

In the beginning, the biggest challenge I faced was where to put everyone. In addition to the barracks that had been built for soldiers, the casements were used for housing. With the exception of the privileged—members of the Council of Elders, their staff, and selected individuals who, because of prestige, were considered prominents—there was a complete separation of families. Those families fortunate enough to remain intact lived in small one- or two-room apartments called *kumbals*. Most of the men, sometimes as many as 6,000, lived in the gigantic Sudeten barracks with up to 300 in one room. The rest of the male population resided in Hannover and other smaller barracks where the quarters were no less overcrowded.

As many as 250 men might find themselves living in a single barracks with their own individual space being about two and a half feet in width, containing their bed and, with luck, any luggage they still possessed. Like everything else in my dominion, these suitcases were put to good use by standing them vertically to provide for a bit of privacy. What bedding was provided to each person consisted of a straw mattress, a pillow, and two blankets. In the barracks where three-tier bunks were used for sleeping, the inmates hung whatever sets of extra clothing they had from the bunks.

Women fared even worse. In the female barracks, there were no wooden bedsteads but only mattresses on the floor with one next to the other, forcing the women to tap-dance around the several inches of space separating one mattress from another. From a distance, the bobbing heads and bodies skipping into the air reminded me of a ballet with the music accompaniment left to the imagination.

It was by design that families were broken up. The Germans feared a new generation of Jews hell-bent on exacting revenge, and so every effort was made to remove any opportunity to procreate. If a marriage was shaky at the start, it was destined to deteriorate in my milieu. At best, families could gather for a meal, but then each member was compelled to go his or her separate way, sometimes leaving a wayward spouse in search of a dark corner to have relations with a clandestine lover. On the other hand, more committed husbands frequently bribed the guards of the female barracks with cigarettes to steal a few amorous moments with their wives. But ultimately, most families were broken and torn asunder. When pregnancies did occur, the babies, for the most part, like little Daniel Redlich, never lived to exact retribution.

Naturally in order to work, people needed sustenance to supply the energy to labor. This is simply a matter of common sense, but you wouldn't know it from the rationing and food supply the German authorities instituted. The daily ration of 1,600 calories did not allow for butter, eggs, fat, vegetables, or dairy products. Officially, the food offering included peeled potatoes, sauerkraut, special weekly treats of dumplings and rutabaga, called *dorschen*, meat, doughnuts fried in fat, and a lentil soup that was usually nothing more than water mixed with a touch of lentil abstract with sand blended in to give it substance. The inmates derisively referred to this concoction as *wrucken*. But due to pilferage by the Germans and Czechs, the supplies earmarked for the inmates were severely depleted. Mostly, the people depended on the bread allocation for survival. The loaves were divided in precise portions measured with rulers; more was provided for the laborers and less for the sick and those not working. Ersatz coffee, which afforded temporary warmth to the belly but no nourishment, was frequently all that was served at dinner.

The kitchen was staffed with twenty-five to thirty cooks. At any time, day or night, more than 100 women would be peeling potatoes in eight-hour shifts. Seated and crammed together, hunched over pails into which the peeled potatoes along with the peelings were dropped, the women spent the hours speaking of times past. Though demanding, jobs involving food distribution or preparation were the most sought after because there was always enough to eat, and here and there, a leftover scrap could be snuck outside that might be useful to barter for something else, say a cigar or cigarette, though both were officially *verboten*.

The meals were served from eight stalls three times a day. The main meal was lunch consisting of *wrucken* and a ration of potatoes heated in a stove fueled by rolled up paper that had been wetted down and then air-dried plus any wood chips that could be found. People stood in long lines awaiting their allotment. Patience was thin. In a prior life in another world, these people had been most civil and respectful of rules. But hunger and uncertainty do strange things.

Take the day the food slipped from the shaking plate of an elderly man with trembling hands. A fight broke out as people scrambled to retrieve the scraps from the ground. Spotting the mayhem, with thick eyebrows raised, was Ernst Pollatschek, a forty-nine-year-old Czech, the overseer of food distribution, who watched over his domain with dedication and insisted upon as much efficiency as possible. Like a hawk, he could be seen circling the lines, and at the first sign of trouble, he'd dispatch one of his four assistants.

But on this day, Pollatschek did not wait; he jumped into the fracas himself. With his short mustache bristling and his arms thrashing, he pushed people aside, steadying the shaking old man and screaming at the onlookers, "Step back! Back, I say, or they'll be no food for anyone today!" Despite the grumbling, Pollatschek held up the line and prepared a second helping, setting it in the quaking hands of the old man, to replace what had been lost. Only then did the line move on, and the day's meal was ladled onto the plates in a silence so still that the clang of the ladle on the metal plates could be heard echoing off the stone walls.

Hunger is an odd thing. Its causes are varied; its effects on the body and soul can be extreme or a mere nuisance; it can vanish almost instantly or linger like an unwanted relative at a holiday dinner. Hunger can also be the foil to the character of a person.

The vast majority of the inmates had never experienced hunger before, except in the twilight hours nearing the end of the Day of Atonement when they might be chanting the final prayers in a synagogue beneath an ornate ceiling or reading a book or newspaper in the sanctum of a study at home. Interestingly enough, whether out of habit, conscience, or as an act of defiance, most of my residents, regardless of the degree to which they had previously been religiously observant, continued to comply with the Yom Kippur fast and, to the extent they could, stuffed themselves before and after the sundown-to-sundown time of abstinence.

But in my realm, given the diet afforded, hunger was a more gradual and sinister process. I came to learn that the real pains of hunger, the sort where the belly is in a state of constant aching even when one is asleep, do not begin until the third or even the fourth month when a plateau is reached. And then the body resigns itself, and one becomes accustomed to it. Sometimes, there are those who turn this adversity into a triumph of the spirit. Such a woman was Mina Pachter.

Mina was a Czech Jew and already a grandmother when she declined to leave for Palestine with her daughter's family in 1939. Making their good-byes, she had smiled at her daughter, declaring, "You don't move an old tree." Then, as a way of reassuring everyone, and perhaps herself as well, she added, "Besides, who will do anything to old people!"

Perhaps hardest of all was saying good-bye to her grandson David. Leaning down, she gazed at her pride and joy, brushing her fingers through his dark hair lying over his forehead. To David, she must have looked the same as she always had with her streaked-gray hair wavy in the front and piled in the back. Mina set her fleshy cheek by David's face so he could give her a good-bye kiss. He laughed as he did, and she parted her lips into a slight smile, unaware she would never see her family again.

During her stay with me, Mina arranged a cookbook of recipes. Several were hers, but most were contributed by her fellow inmates. Whether due to illness, an interruption, or being summoned for transport, not all recipes were complete, and some were even confusing. The recipes were eclectic and many not even kosher. But they all represented an expression of hope that one day, they would be read and followed, the food prepared, and the meal enjoyed.

Mina compiled her collection of recipes into a hand-sewn copybook that, unlike her and almost all the contributors, would survive the war. Decades later, the threadbare tome made its way into the hands of her daughter living in New York. Ironically, Mina died on Yom Kippur 1944. But the recipes lived on and were published around the world as testimony to the will of the women who contributed them.

Diets barely above the level of starvation made almost everyone susceptible to illness, and as a result, the Jewish Administration was ever mindful of minimizing the spread of disease. Wherever there were toilets, individual ones or latrines, there was a washbasin at the door, and everyone was required to wash their hands. The toilet guards kept a cautious eye and enforced this regulation. The antiquated sewer system, which was designed to service a tenth of the Jewish population, would have been hopelessly clogged were it not for the twenty-two men whose job it was to maintain the flow.

By the end of 1943, I became a full-fledged city with 2,000 water faucets, 1,500 toilets, several kitchens, and a bakery where professional Jewish bakers rolled the dough. I had a laundry, about two dozen shops offering second-hand and ready-to-wear clothing and other goods, a library as impressive as any that could be found in the cities from where my people hailed, a café facing the main square, and a bank located in the former town hall where the officials were instructed by the Director, the former head of the Viennese Jewish community, to maintain assiduous records of fictitious salaries no one earned.

The Council of Elders issued ghetto currency with a sketch of Moses holding the Ten Commandments on one side and the amount of the currency such as *zwanzig kronen* on the other. This worthless money embarrassed me to no end because the sham was shamelessly carried out by my residents. There was absolutely nothing the money could buy; even more insulting was that a bookkeeping system was maintained with the inmates provided valueless accounts from which no money could be withdrawn. The script was useful for the Nazis, however, who made certain it was seen by the Red Cross commission during their visit to foster the illusion the Jews were paid for their labor.

Given the conditions and severely limited supplies, I took great pride in my medical facilities staffed with dedicated physicians and nurses. I still can see Martha Wygodzinski, the former chief physician at a charity hospital for unwed mothers in Berlin, making her rounds on crippled feet, ill with diarrhea, and suffering from the typhus that eventually killed her.

None of this would have been possible were it not for the Jewish Administration and the diligence with which everyone took to their assigned jobs. Each person was issued a labor identity card listing their work assignment which they had to carry at all times. Because there was no private property, and even relatives could not inherit individual belongings, everyone soon realized they were in this hell together. The people were consistently reminded of this state of affairs and exhorted to dedicate themselves to the work ethic by their leaders such as the time Dr. Paul Epstein, the second person to lead the Council of Elders, stood before 2,000 people celebrating the high holy days and, in his deliberate, calming voice, emphasized that survival can only be achieved with the strongest work effort. No talk. Perform your duties. Work.

Everything about me was organized. Daily life was largely unchanged from one sunrise to another: wake up in a cold, dreary room; wash your hands and face with ice-cold water; walk at dawn to receive lukewarm ersatz coffee and bread; work with a pause for lunch and maybe an afternoon nap if you're old; then a last meal possibly followed by an evening lecture or performance with curfew no later than nine.

There was a distinct protocol to follow. The German authorities dealt only with the Council of Elders, wittingly leaving the impression to the populace that the Council actually made policy when, in fact, they were merely puppets hanging from taut German strings. The Council officially communicated with the general population by issuing the Orders of the Day, which was a bit of a misnomer since they often were only released every several days. In addition to directives and other information, the Orders published the punishments of those inmates found guilty of violating the rules—most frequently stealing for which the sentences ranged from days to months in detention.

Rules were enforced by the Jewish police, or Ghetto Guard. Though some of the guards did not take themselves very seriously since they had no weapons, others went about their duties strutting with shoulders squared, solemn demeanors, and staring from unsmiling faces. These men could be seen watching over the warehouses and privies, adorned in leather or cloth belts with cross belts over the shoulders and visor caps perched on their heads.

The somberness with which the guards conducted themselves reflected the attitude of the Director of Security Services, Dr. Karl Lowenstein, a fifty-year-old stocky and energetic man as well as a loyal German who had been a high-ranking officer in the Great War. He organized his troops, numbering as many as 450 men, in precise military formation. I can see why many of the people scoffed at, and sometimes even opposed, the power Lowenstein took upon himself. Indeed, when, on the second anniversary of the Guard's existence, Lowenstein headed a parade with the men marching through the courtyards decked out in their new, gray-green uniform jackets with two pockets left and right, many in the crowd wearing tattered clothing were more than resentful. Yet I myself, as well as many members of the Council, appreciated how much Lowenstein dedicated himself to his work.

Before the Nazi regime and the Nuremberg laws were enacted, Lowenstein had been a lawyer who turned to banking, so he was accustomed to wielding authority. Therefore, it was only natural that when given command of the guard, he envisioned himself to be in the epicenter of power, believing his mission was to fight corruption.

In his personal life, Lowenstein could be most charming. When guests came to visit, something he encouraged for he was, after all, a social man, he graciously ushered them into his private room which was filled with modern furniture. Smiling, he would point out a place to be seated. From the kitchen area, he brewed some tea which he served accompanied by a sliver of cake. Seating himself and, from time to time, sipping a bit of tea, Lowenstein would animatedly engage in conversation ranging over a variety of topics from ghetto concerns to when the War might end.

But on the job, the Director of Security Services was vigilant. Forgoing the official uniform and wearing a nondescript blue suit and cap, Lowenstein blended in with the masses so he could pop up out of nowhere, ensuring that his guards were alert. To expect compassion or leniency from such a man would be foolhardy, something young Ludwig Troller was to learn.

Ah yes, Ludwig, the nephew of Norbert Troller, one of the artists who paid with their lives creating work depicting the chilling story of my existence—something I will relate later. Consequently, I was especially disposed to young Ludwig, but I probably would have been so inclined anyway. After all, who could not have been seduced by this handsome young man always in high spirits, loved by many, especially the women which regrettably proved his undoing?

One of the ladies Ludwig charmed had a jealous boyfriend. As I have said, human passions were merely diminished, not eradicated, within my walls. Coincidentally, and most unfortunately for Ludwig, he and the aggrieved boyfriend were both members of the Ghetto Guard. When the boyfriend learned that Ludwig had accepted contraband from a Czech gendarme, not an uncommon practice, he reported the matter to Lowenstein. Lowenstein was known for not tolerating even a single infraction amongst his troops. Despite pleas from friends, family, and even the Council of Elders, he remained intransigent in the matter involving Ludwig Troller and would make no exception. With his burly torso held rigid, Lowenstein pronounced his decision once and for all; the young man was neither fit to wear the uniform of the Ghetto Guard nor be spared exemption from transport. It was only a matter of time before young Ludwig, crestfallen and shoulders slumped, was dispatched on a transport east where, upon his arrival, he was shot.

Outside of lording over his troops, Lowenstein's power was limited to enforcing the rules. Ferreting out those who violated the regulations was left to the Department of Criminal Investigations headed by Dr. Ernst Rosenthal. Probably reflecting the German penchant for organization and proper procedure, a bureaucracy was established befitting the world imagined by Franz Kafka, whose sister Ottla, by the way, was a resident of mine in 1943.

Ottla was a beautiful woman. Her black hair was brushed back and short enough that the bottom halves of her ears were visible. Dark eyebrows served as the canopy above deep, penetrating eyes. Thin lips seemed to always be shaped into a slight smile below a prominent nose.

But it was not because she was striking and the sister of Franz Kafka that I remember Ottla so well; rather, it was because she was a most courageous human being. Once she understood the fate of Europe's Jews, Ottla separated from her husband, who was a gentile, claiming she had no right to avoid the suffering of her people. For this, she was rewarded with a trip to my domain where she worked with children who were often sick. In 1943, when a trainload of children was ordered to be sent to an unknown destination, Ottla volunteered to accompany them to allay their anxiety. The destination turned out to be Auschwitz. Like her sisters, Ottla was murdered by the Germans.

But I have digressed, something I find myself apt to do with so many names and faces and souls floating within my consciousness. So permit me to return to the bureaucracy in my realm as it was encountered by Philipp Manes. Manes was a fastidious man who single-handedly organized 500 cultural events during the time he spent with me. One day, Manes noticed that his shoe was in need of repair. Although it was only a matter of a few stitches to reconnect the upper leather to the sole, he learned he must first obtain a coupon from the Labor Exchange before proceeding to the shoe repair shop. This meant standing in line in a room packed with people petitioning for requests of all sorts. Upon finally reaching the front, he made his application. The round-faced lady listened patiently, smiled, and said, "Come back in ten days. Permits and coupons will be issued at that time. Until then, there is too much backlog in the repair shop." Resigned, Manes shrugged and sauntered away.

Not long thereafter, Manes realized his winter coat wouldn't do in the summer, so once again he made an application, this time for a lightweight jacket. Informed that an investigator would be assigned his case to examine his belongings to see if there was, indeed, a need, he waited patiently. Of course, by the time he obtained the authorization, it was no longer summer, and the approaching cold weather meant it would soon be time for his winter coat again.

While the bureaucracy could prove daunting, the organization of my realm did result in an effective work force which improved the odds for survival. Everyone over the age of fourteen was expected to work. At first, all able-bodied persons were employed in building habitable quarters. Once this was accomplished, and everyone secured a place to sleep, the attics were thoroughly cleaned and used for concerts, dramas, operas, lectures, and other cultural events organized by people like Manes. With living quarters attained, attention focused on establishing a habitable environment, and to do this, individuals were assigned to one of three groups: working in construction or agriculture; providing a labor force for a number of important economic fields; or internal maintenance, which included unskilled labor.

A word about this so-called unskilled labor force. Do not for a moment think that those consigned to this category lacked intelligence or talent. It is simply that what they had to contribute to their new society was not practical. What good was the negotiating skill of a cattle merchant when there was no market for cattle? Or the knowledge of the working mechanics of motorcars when the only means of transportation was the pushcarts employed to convey the fresh supply of corpses for disposal? And what of the proficiency of the *hausfrau* when one's home is reduced to a cot with barely enough space to walk around the perimeter? How many accountants were needed to balance the books in my bank of sham accounts funded by useless currency? Or lawyers to prepare wills for people who had nothing to bequeath after their deaths? Is it, therefore, a surprise that so many people who had once taken much pride in their lives before tramping through my ramparts were devastated when they were declared to be unskilled? Or that they viewed with disdain what they were compelled to do? People like Mariánka Zadikow, who complained about the "very dirty and very disagreeable job, mostly cleaning something uncleanable with nothing but buckets, cold water, brushes, rags, and absolutely no soap or detergents."

True, this sense of indignation paled in comparison to the mortal fear felt whenever the word transport was mentioned or to the persistent ache of hunger and constant cold and dampness that permeated every inch of one's body. But make no mistake; for most of my people, the sense of self-worth they might have possessed before entering my world was stripped away in the most abrupt and callous manner when the label unskilled was affixed beside any of their names.

All new arrivals were assigned to menial jobs involving maintenance, though after a month, an application could be made to the Central Labor Office for another position. Most sought after was the agricultural work because that meant leaving my imposing granite walls, attaining a respite from the chilly, dank air and being jostled by the throngs scuttling to and fro. Instead, one could walk freely, perhaps with a hoe balanced over the shoulder, squinting up at the sunlit blue sky and inhaling fresh air. But this was only for the more fortunate.

There were departments providing all sorts of services to make the people believe they lived in a city even if not one of their own choosing: repair shops for everything useful, from fixing the few creaking hearses which, at first, were the only vehicles available for transport, to revamping wheelchairs needed by the infirm and those disabled in the Great War; constructing new carriages for transportation; wood-working shops assembling windows, frames, doors, benches, and chairs; carpentry shops. There even existed a department that produced high-quality furniture for the SS and a ceramics industry that crafted dolls sought by the SS to send to their children.

Within my domain, my people did everything. Former lawyers, professors, bankers, and merchants were engaged in laying water pipes, paving roads, drilling wells, cleaning sewers, sweeping streets, and changing electric wires. There was some compensation to being assigned more strenuous work: one received larger food rations. The stokers, builders, porters, and sewage workers were given 500 grams of bread per day while ordinary workers were allotted 375 grams, and those unable to work at all were provided only 335 grams.

Women who had once been *hausfraus* or teachers or shopkeepers spent their hours baking bread, weaving baskets, milking cows, and raising silkworms. People did what life demanded to maintain my realm. They worked.

It did not take long for the German Authority to realize they had an excellent resource to aid in the War effort—a captive workforce, so to say. And once this became known, the Council realized they had some value to the Germans other than providing more Jewish corpses. As early as the summer of 1942, up to 200 women were assigned to separate feldspar, which the Germans used for insulation in arms production. By the middle of 1943, leather was made for boots and goggles; uniforms were mended; cardboard boxes were constructed to hold ammunition; and up to 1,000 inmates assembled protective crates with insulation to prevent German engines from freezing on the Russian front.

Alas, death demanded perhaps the most attention from the workforce. An unidentified barracks served as a facility where the coffins were piled four and five feet high. The deceased of the previous day were put in coffins the next morning and then placed in freshly dug graves. Expeditiousness was critical not only because the Jewish religion required a prompt burial, but no one wanted so many unburied coffins filled with bodies serving as a stark and vivid reminder of what might lay in store.

At one time or another, every able-bodied man had to serve a turn as a grave digger. When it became clear, late in 1942, that there was a scarcity of ground to meet the need, a crematorium was built, which spared the expense of constructing coffins and also saved wood for other purposes. Ashes were placed in cardboard boxes with the pertinent information noted on each box, and a registry was maintained.

Fifty thousand souls were freed from their corporeal remains in the crematorium—almost one of every three Jews who trudged beneath the *Arbeit Macht Frei* icon. Ironically, the Nazis were right; the work did liberate the Jewish souls from this earth. In the end, all the ashes were lost to the ages.

CHAPTER THREE: THE COUNCIL OF ELDERS

From the moment I first breathed in the cold, clammy air encased by my granite walls, each and every Jewish soul passing under my archway and entering my corporeal realm became a part of my ethereal existence. I knew them all and still do, though some more than others. This is only natural.

Of course, those who were famous and well-known became etched more firmly into my memory and consciousness. Many of these people were distinguished by the title of prominents and were classified as such by the German Authority. At any given time, there were a hundred or so prominents; they were mostly German or Austrian Jews who, in one way or another, were deemed by the German Authority to be above the parasitic nature of all the other Jews. One might have attained this status by having held a high military rank or government office or, perhaps, having been in charge of a major business or bank. Conceivably, it could have been nothing more fortuitous than having given birth to the illegitimate sons of royalty or being born the bastard granddaughter of a famous composer. All of this was true, so I never bothered much with these people who enjoyed privileges regarding living quarters, rations, and exemption from work duties.

On the other hand, those who achieved renown because of what they accomplished during their time spent with me … well, that is another matter entirely, and I have taken each one to my heart. I have already spoken of some of these folks, and many more will follow, but for now, I want to reflect upon three men in particular who, at one time or another, served as the leader of the Council of Elders.

All the members of the Council of Elders had certain benefits associated with their role, somewhat similar to the prominents. The families of the Council and their staff were not sent to dormitory living quarters but remained intact. Their sparsely furnished individual rooms in the Magdeburg barracks were small and gloomy and faced inward toward the hallway. Nonetheless, they were envied by everyone else because they, at least, enjoyed privacy and much-desired possessions, such as an iron stove, an electric hot plate, chairs and a table, a lamp, individual beds, or perhaps even a mirror! They ate special food, and a cleaning staff washed their floors and laundered their clothes. The Elder of the Jews, the head of the Council, resided in a two-room flat with windows looking out on the street.

But whether these benefits were worth the attendant responsibilities and duties remained to be seen, given the Herculean and sometimes impossible assignments the German Authority fully expected to be implemented with the utmost efficiency. The Council's primary task was to enact regulations to govern the Jewish city, enforced by a legal system and police force. These laws were in addition to the edicts established by the Germans which governed every aspect of camp life and from which there was no appeal. However, the enforcement of the Jewish laws, always subject to German approval, was conducted by Jewish jurists in formal hearings.

What were some of the infractions and punishments meted out? Hermann Gross was sentenced to ten days' imprisonment and a day without warm food for stealing provisions from the kitchen where he worked. Alfred Reichmann was sentenced to three weeks' imprisonment for pushing another resident, causing her to fall and injure her ankle. Julius Lappert served three weeks in prison for stealing a winter coat. But the impressive thing that made me very proud of my people who were living under such horrific conditions was that during the first year, not one single murder was committed nor were any incidents of rape, robbery, or violence charged. Of the 5,200 violations, all were either crimes of theft or offenses against regulations. What other city of so large a population can make such a claim?

Unlike the German jail, the Little Fortress, from which few ever emerged, the Jewish prisons were less crowded than the barracks, and the Jewish guards were friendly. Consequently, in a sense, a prison sentence was often no punishment at all. Decent rations, no work, and a bit of space to be alone. Almost a vacation! But the stigma and shame of being sent to prison was difficult to bear. If nothing else, most of my people tenaciously clung to their pride.

On the other hand, the stress on the nerves was considerable to those incarcerated because, at times, the prisons were emptied to fill transports headed east. After a year, additional courts were established to handle labor disputes, civil disputes among the residents, and even an administrative court to resolve complaints filed against the staff for failure to follow regulations. There was never a lack of experienced jurists willing to serve the legal system.

Initially, the Council was to be an advisory board with its members and large staff consisting of fifty to 100 people representative of a cross-section of the population. However, a consensus did not come easily. It pains me that there were factions among my people, especially since to me, all Jews are the same. As I saw it, on the one hand, there were the Jews, and on the other hand, there was everyone else—the German soldiers and SS, Czech gendarmes, all of them murderers and criminals. But the Jews saw things differently, creating divisions based mostly on nationalities; there were the Czech Jews and the German Jews and the Austrian Jews and then came the Dutch Jews and the Hungarian ... Enough!

In the beginning, all the Jews hailed from the Protectorate, so it was only natural that the original members of the Council were all Czech Jews. In December of 1941, after the vanguard of workers and administrators had arrived, followed by the first transport filled with my future occupants, the reins of administration were transferred to the twelve-man Council headed by thirty-eight-year-old Jakob Edelstein.

One of Edelstein's chief functions was to act as liaison between the German commandant and the Council. Indeed, Edelstein met every day except Sunday with the German commandant—a man who, at a whim, could make his life miserable and even end it altogether. In the beginning, this man was Dr. Siegfried Seidl whom Edelstein would later look back upon with a sense of perverse longing after Seidl was replaced by Anton Burger. In place of Seidl's sublime sadism, Burger was a brazen brute.

During these meetings, Edelstein reported on the status of the ghetto, the number of sick, and progress made on previous instructions. Occasionally, he might dare to make a few suggestions and requests, but he would only do so if he sensed that the commandant might be receptive and was in a good mood. Such days were infrequent. Most mornings, at one point or another while Edelstein recited his report, a fist would smash on the table like the clap of thunder accompanied by a shriek and the hurling of German invectives. After a moment's pause, Edelstein would continue in a tenuous voice; he'd occasionally glance up and brace himself for another round if he sighted the formation of sneering lips and darkening eyes heralding the approach of a second and perhaps even more devastating storm. However, if Edelstein did determine it was one of those days when he might proceed to submit an application, he would always do so in a quiet intonation and subservient demeanor, bending forward as a sign of respect to the man seated across from him, carefully and diplomatically choosing his words so the commandant might later think the idea emanated from himself and himself alone.

Edelstein might have dared to be a bit bolder if it were not for the fact that there was more at stake than his own life when he met with the commandant. After all, he had to consider his family who had joined him shortly after his arrival: Miriam, his wife and four years his junior; their eleven-year-old son, Arieh, a boy with long, spindly legs who was thin even before being subjected to my Spartan diet; and Miriam's mother, Mrs. Olliner. Unlike her husband who had always concerned himself with business and Zionism, Miriam, a delicate woman with attentive, large, brown eyes, loved music and the theater. Her vocation had been teaching English in high school. Perhaps this might be useful after the War, she sometimes considered, for who knew where they would land?

But do not take any of this to mean that Jakob Edelstein was the Nazi's lackey. It's just that he knew a frontal assault would prove fruitless and be self-destructive. Edelstein never hesitated to lie to the Germans, to conceal, to commit covert sabotage, anything to save a Jewish life, and the people realized this. He would cover up the smuggling that was rampant in the ghetto and conceal attempted escapes. While the German Authority mockingly referred to Edelstein as the King of the Jews, most of the population held him in high regard, believing he was doing the best he could.

How the people felt about him was very important to Jakob, though he kept it to himself. The German barbs stung him, and he was afraid the people mocked him behind his back or, even worse, believed him to be inept and unwilling to stand up for them. But he dared not ask anyone directly about this concern, and as with human nature, rarely did anyone volunteer to thank him for what he was doing, though no one hesitated to grumble a complaint or bombard him with just one more request.

So when the opportunity to tactfully inquire from someone who was objective and on whom he could rely for an honest answer, he seized it. This took place well into his tenure in the summer of 1943 with the arrival of Bedriska Hostovska, a woman he had known from his work in the community education division back in Prague.

One day, to her surprise, Bedriska was summoned from her quarters, an attic that she shared with 100 other women, to see Edelstein in his office. The pleasantries were brief because Bedriska knew there was a reason she had been called by the Elder, and she was anxious to know what it could be.

"Tell me, Bedriska," Edelstein hesitantly said, "What do the ghetto veterans say to the newcomers like you about things … things here … in the ghetto?"
Bedriska shrugged and finally asked, "Such as?"

"Oh, many things … anything … even about me. How do they feel about me?"

"Oh, only good things are said about you, Jakob!" Bedriska exclaimed. "You're well thought of." Edelstein let out a sigh of relief before Bedriska's puzzled expression.

"You must know, Bedriska, everyone must know that I would never sign anything that could harm my people." Edelstein looked intently and imploringly into Bedriska's eyes, grasping her hand in his. There was a knock, and then the door opened upon the weary face of Leo Janowitz, Edelstein's right-hand man. Although only thirty, Janowitz was selected as Edelstein's chief deputy because he had been his secretary at the Prague Palestine office where they both had dedicated themselves arranging for Jews to settle in the Holy Land. Always quiet and introverted by nature, Leo spoke even more sparingly in my milieu, as though he could never find the right words to respond to situations that were so unexpected, so unique, so unanticipated that a new language demanded to be invented. With a nod of his long, stately face toward the line of people, Janowitz ushered Bedriska from the room.

I held a strong fondness for Jakob for another reason as well. Too many of the prominents and members of the Council behaved high-handedly. Some went to great lengths to procure special furnishings to make their tiny flats impressive without ever feeling the slightest pang of guilt in having it so much better than everyone else. But Jakob was not like this at all. His two-room flat was modestly furnished, and the door was always left open so people could come and go at all hours, which they frequently did.

Edelstein was always courteous, and he would greet people in the streets, sometimes stopping and chatting for as long as his frenzied schedule would allow before dashing off to attend to some urgent or not-so-urgent problem. He could be seen hatless with his wavy, black hair blowing in the wind as he sprinted through my streets.

Some of the residents wondered why he did not have a hat on during the frigid days of winter. Few knew that Edelstein avoided wearing a hat, as I mentioned earlier, because it excused him from lifting his hat whenever a German was near, as was required. He very much enjoyed speaking at public forums, and he made for an effective and enjoyable speaker because his sincerity was so apparent.

The composition of the Council and the demographics of my denizens underwent a dramatic change in the summer of 1942 when the city was "officially" handed over to the Jews by the German Authority, and the SS were rarely visible. While many people were relieved at the physical absence of the SS, I was not. Indeed, human emotions were being infused into my constitution, and I felt different, being more fearful of the threat from what cannot be seen, what lurks in the shadows. I'd rather have my enemies in plain sight.

It was at this time the German and Austrian Jews began arriving, thus necessitating a change in the personnel of the Council. The German Authority mandated that half the members be from this new group with two from Austria and four from Germany. The two from Vienna were Desider Friedmann, the former president of the Viennese Jewish community and his assistant, Robert Stricker. Of the four German Jews, Heinrich Stahl, former chairman of Berlin's Jewish community, was the most distinguished, and he became Edelstein's deputy. Edelstein retained his position as Elder of the Jews.

Given the altered composition of the Council and the specious role I was to play as a resort-town where elderly German Jews could live out their lives in tranquility, it was destined that Edelstein would be replaced as head of the Council of Elders. Moreover, although loathing all Jews, the Germans preferred their own Jews to the rest of the vile race, hence making the change inevitable that a German Jew would lead the Council.

Do not take this personally, Eichmann began in a half-hearted attempt to pacify Edelstein as he informed him in January of 1943 that he was to be replaced by Dr. Paul Epstein, the previous head of the Reich Union of Jews in Germany, who would now lead a triumvirate along with Edelstein and Lowenherz from Vienna. Edelstein managed to retain his composure before the chiseled face and stiff figure seated opposite him, but inside, he seethed. How could he not take this personally! Indeed, Edelstein was deeply hurt, and he respectfully requested that he be relieved of all his duties as a member of the Council and assigned to work as a menial laborer.

But Eichmann refused, dismissing this as nonsense with the wave of a hand and an insidious sparkle in his eyes.

To make matters worse for Edelstein, he deemed Epstein to be totally unqualified as his replacement. This probably had a lot to do with the fact that Epstein was the antithesis of Edelstein. Herr Doktor Epstein preferred being addressed formally, an honor he earned having been educated in philosophy, sociology, and political economics as well as attaining the rank of assistant professor at the age of twenty-five—no minor achievement for a Jew in Germany. Certainly, Epstein's rarified milieu of academia was a stark contrast to the rough-and-tumble world of commerce and hands-on Zionism that Edelstein had once inhabited.

There were other differences as well. Edelstein was an affable man and loved having people around him whereas Epstein was a loner, reticent and unreceptive. I already have spoken of Edelstein's open-door policy at all hours of the day and night—a stark contrast to Epstein's established visitation hours between four and five in the afternoon. This is not a university where Herr Professor sets office hours for students, Edelstein fumed to himself. He seriously doubted that his successor could withstand the pressure of the job.

But some people have a way to manage the strain of their responsibilities by compensating with pleasurable activities, and this was Epstein's solution. He was a man much influenced by Western culture who loved music and was a skilled pianist himself. Epstein was so taken in with the pretense served up to German Jewry about my function as a resort-like retirement community that he actually arranged to have his grand piano transported into my domain whereupon arrival, it could be seen carted through my streets and into his quarters. Many an evening, one might hear poignant melodies drifting from the Epstein residence where some of Europe's most gifted musicians performed concerts for select audiences.

Herr Doktor Paul Epstein was, above all, a man of honor who prided himself in his integrity. Unfortunately for my people, this meant that unlike Edelstein, he would not even entertain the notion of falsifying records or sabotaging German orders. Indeed, he always carried on his person a dose of cyanide to end his life should the Germans try to force him to act in a manner that was inconsistent with his code of honor.

However, all the privileges, power, and prestige could not compensate for the oppressive burden borne by the Council members when they had to compile the transport lists dispatching thousands to an uncertain fate if not their deaths. I will dwell on this later, and the longer I can put off recounting those terrible hours leading to filling the trains, the better. I mention it here, however, because more than anything else, this is what led to Edelstein's demise.

On November 9, 1943, Edelstein was summoned to an interrogation—his own. Although this was unprecedented, he was not surprised. Indeed, for some time, Edelstein had felt the probing eyes of the SS peering over his shoulder and searing his back. He imagined these sinister silhouettes in their long leather trench coats, the smoke emanating from their cigarettes drifting down dim alleys and murky corners where they secreted themselves and watched. He believed the SS were everywhere, lurking in the darkness, and he had sensed for some time that he was the subject of surveillance.

What did bewilder Edelstein, however, was that the examination was conducted by a mere SS officer and not Commandant Burger himself, so perhaps it was nothing to be anxious about, he contemplated. At first, the line of questioning focused upon his involvement in the escape of Jewish residents. Prisoners! Inmates! I wanted to correct the German imbecile because by definition, residents were people free to come and go at will where my denizens were not. Edelstein could not have been concerned very much about this issue because few inmates ever escaped, and those who did had succeeded by bribing Czech guards who probably kicked back to the SS—possibly the very man conducting the interview.

No, more than complicity in a handful of missing Jews was needed to bring down Edelstein. The real ammunition in the German Luger would be found in the records that were meticulously maintained by the Council staff; after all, who better than the Germans, well known for their proficiency at record keeping, to unearth any errors. Speaking barely above a whisper, the SS interrogator mentioned that there seemed to be a discrepancy involving fifty-five names of people boarding the transports east. The problem in these cases is that all fifty-five had been recorded as dead before the trains left the station. How can someone who is listed as dead board a train two weeks later? The SS officer feigned incomprehension. I'd like to know how to do this, Herr Edelstein, he said with a sneer spreading across his face. It would certainly be useful to the War effort if we could bring back our fallen soldiers to fight another day! The SS officer snickered.

Edelstein was caught, and he knew it. Of course, there must have been other reasons to want him out of the way, for what were fifty-five Jewish lives when tens of thousands of my people had already died. But for Edelstein, each life he could save meant everything, and he didn't regret what he had done. But to the Germans? What was a Jewish life? Nothing.

The next day, along with Feltyn Goldschmied and Egon Deutsch, both clerks in the record department, Edelstein was arrested. Edelstein's fate remained uncertain for many weeks, but by mid-December, the German intentions regarding what to do with the first Elder of the Jews became clear. The Council was ordered to compile a transit list of 5,000 Czech Jews and to include the Edelstein family.

Deep down, Jakob had never believed he would survive the War, though he kept this hidden very well. But he did believe his son, Arieh, would make it through, and everything he did had this in mind. He had even harbored the hope that his son was destined for greatness, and while he might not be able to use his influence and position to save himself, and possibly not even his wife, his son would survive. But all this was cruelly shattered when among the 2,500 men, women, and children boarding the first transport on Wednesday, December 15 were the ashen faces of Miriam and Arieh Edelstein along with Miriam's mother, Mrs. Olliner.

It wasn't clear whether Jakob would board the same transport as his family, but it was assumed he would. Most people on the train that day expected that Jakob Edelstein, just like Moses, would lead these thousands of exiled Jews to their new home, a labor camp where they could still prove their value to the Third Reich and thus remain alive. They trusted that he would organize everyone and create a productive community just as he did within my walls. At least, this is what Miriam and Jakob and most others had hoped. But when Jakob Edelstein, the man who had been most responsible to establish the façade of an independent Jewish city in Hitler's thousand-year Reich, was surreptitiously scooted onto the last car of the train—the car reserved for prisoners—this illusion fell by the wayside along with thousands of other decimated dreams and delusions.

I wish I could say with certainty exactly how Edelstein and his family fared for the next six months. Were they brutally beaten or perhaps accorded a modicum of respect? Did they struggle under conditions of forced labor, or were they allowed some exemption from the work details that were designed to kill? Did they still cling to any hope they might survive? Jakob was so integral to my very quintessence that I sometimes feel I know the answers to these questions, and yet, how can I be sure? After all, I was not there, and all I know for certain is what I can see and hear and absorb in my own space and own time.

What I do know of the Edelstein family's fate comes from a Polish prisoner at Auschwitz who entered my realm in June 1945 and made inquiries about the man whose face appeared on our currency—Jakob Edelstein. He said that he knew the man and witnessed his death in Auschwitz. This is what I learned.

Upon the Edelstein family's arrival, Jakob was placed in punishment block 11 while Miriam, Arieh, and Mrs. Olliner were assigned to the family camp. The family camp had been established primarily to foster the charade that the Jews from my realm who boarded the transports heading east were not being dispatched to their deaths. In reality, it merely provided a temporary stay of execution.

For half a year, the Edelstein family remained alive. But on June 20, 1944, an SS car pulled up with orders to collect Edelstein. In curt words, the SS officer informed Jakob that he had been sentenced to death. To the consternation of the SS officer, Edelstein took his time shaking hands with his cellmates. Finally, the SS man demanded Edelstein be swift, to which Jakob bravely replied, "I am master of my last moments." But alas, like everything else those past few years, Edelstein was anything but master of his moments.

Immediately after dropping off Edelstein at crematorium number 3, the SS car drove to the family camp and retrieved the Edelstein family: Miriam, Arieh, and Mrs. Olliner. Though debilitated with diphtheria, Miriam bolted from her bed, so anxious was she to see her husband. But she collapsed after staggering down the corridor and had to be brought to the car on a stretcher. The family was driven to crematorium 3 where they joined Jakob. The reunion was brief. The Nazis were efficient. Killing needed to be done, and it was to be swift.

Before Jacob could object, cajole, plead, or perhaps even pray; before his very own eyes, eyes that could not deceive him nor make the reality go away, Mrs. Olliner and Miriam were shot amidst derisive remarks from their killers. There followed a moment's respite, a moment of faith, an instant to believe that some decency remained in the world, a moment that ignited just a flicker of hope that his son might be spared. But then, more contemptuous comments and another blast of the pistol, leaving his Arieh lying dead not far from his feet, lifeless, eyes and mouth wide open—perhaps looking and pleading for his father to help. How could Jakob have withstood this? I've often grappled with how he lived his last moments. No being should ever have to bear witness to such a thing. What reason was there left to live? He must have yearned for death to be united with his loved ones, to be released from the pain—the wrenching pain like nothing he had ever felt in his life—to be allowed to die.

The Nazi killers swiftly obliged. Jakob Edelstein was shot. Death came instantly.

• • •

The day after Edelstein's arrest, Dr. Paul Epstein became the head of the Council of Elders. His first assistant was Otto Zucker who assumed the unofficial post of spokesman for the Czech Jews. Epstein's initial assignment from Commandant Burger was to prepare a marching plan to evacuate the entire ghetto so a general census could be taken. Whether or not the errant fifty-five names in the records the Germans uncovered was the reason for Edelstein's arrest and the undertaking of a census was not known to Epstein, and he was certainly not about to question it. He was determined, however, to carry out the order and see to it that the ghetto was emptied efficiently and as quickly as possible.

This would be no easy task. Only the bedridden, pregnant women, and prisoners were exempt which left 40,000 people to pass out from under my archway to the outside world. They would do so with precision and according to Epstein's plan, gathering street by street in groups of 100 and marching five abreast. At six in the morning, the evacuation commenced. The day was typical for the middle of November: severely cold and damp. The leafless trees blended into the gray skies. People were instructed to wear warm clothing and bring food. Some inmates wrapped themselves in blankets against the frigid dawn air, but the mist soon made everything wet—their coats, their blankets, even their exposed skin.

By 9:30, everyone was in place, and people began moving out past the walls which had imprisoned them for months. The fact a world existed beyond their pris-on-fortress-city seemed surreal to most of them. Indeed, for people like Sophie and Ludwig Frank, who had arrived a year earlier with the initial waves of German Jews, the world seemed just as they remembered it. They saw the bare branches of trees bending in the wind; they smelled the exhausts from the buses traversing the roadway to various destinations; they overheard typical morning salutations uttered by the populace dressed in warm, woolen clothing passing each other as they headed off to work or to shop. The clinks of the children skipping on the sidewalk reminded Sophie of her own daughters when they were younger. How she envied these folks living their lives as lives were meant to be lived, not the way she and Ludwig and the other Jews were forced to subsist each day.

Suddenly, Sophie's reverie was shattered by the piercing sound of military aircraft flying overhead, bringing her and everyone else back to reality. It made her take notice of the Czech police armed with rifles surrounding them, the SS riding on bicycles through their ranks, and Burger glaring at the people while astride his black steed, prancing through the throng. As more and more people became aware of the significant military presence, many began to entertain the notion that they were all about to be murdered, and the census was just one more façade to get them to cooperate like marionettes in their own execution.

Ludwig leaned into Sophie with a look of panic in his eyes. She was his strength and had been since he came home from the Great War a victim of mustard gas. Sophie grasped his forearm and squeezed while everyone around her spoke hurriedly in hushed tones trying to reassure one another. Finally, a consensus emerged, concluding the Germans would never murder all these people outside my fortification for all the world to witness. How brazen could they be? If they only knew, I thought to myself, how little attention the world paid to the plight of European Jewry, they would not have dismissed the prospect so easily.

In every respect, save one, the day proved disastrous. Amazingly, the people stood patiently; no one was permitted to sit. Someone began to count, then another; then Epstein took charge with the count, his face pallid and anxious; then the SS became involved counting the people. As the hours passed, here and there, a body slumped to the ground. No one was allowed to pick up the fallen comrade. The person would just lie there. After twenty hours, the task was abandoned, and whatever number had been reached was considered the best obtainable. Orders were given to return to the ghetto. The inmates squeezed through the one narrow opening the Germans desig-nated to be used to re-enter my realm.

But as I had said, there was one noteworthy achievement that day. Given the weak condition and advanced age of so many of my residents, the cold November weather, the stress of the day, and being forced to stand for twenty hours, Burger's census succeeded in killing hundreds of Jews. Ironically enough, this meant that even if the census had been accurate, it became invalid within minutes from the final tally since the deaths had not been deducted.

Herr Doktor Paul Epstein's term as the head of the Council of Elders lasted less than a year, although in my dominion, this equated to an interminable amount of time. The new commandant, Karl Rahm, who replaced Burger in February 1944, had long wanted to rid himself of Epstein. Based on a trumped up charge that he was attempting to escape, on September 27, 1944, Rahm ordered Epstein's arrest. The accusation was absurd on its face, alleging that Epstein had gone to the warehouse which was located outside the gate without having a proper pass to do so. The irony was not lost on Epstein that the person who signed such passes for the inmates was none other than he himself! Was he required to petition himself for a pass that only he could grant to himself? Such was German logic when it came to justifying the murdering of Jews!

Epstein had expected to at least be able to face his accuser, Commandant Rahm, the man who had seen Epstein outside the fortress walls and ordered him arrested. Proper protocol required no less. After all, he was Herr Doktor Paul Epstein, the leader of the entire Jewish community and head of the Council of Elders; no one other than the highest ranking German officer should have the authority to pass any sentence upon him or remove him from office. It violated every established principal of protocol.

But it was only one of Rahm's underlings who appeared at Epstein's door reading the charge in the manner of a bored policeman reciting a traffic citation. He demanded, he did not request, that Epstein accompany him immediately. That day was the last time anyone ever saw the second Elder of the Jews—except for the man who shot Epstein in the back somewhere on the grounds of the Little Fortress.

Dr. Benjamin Murmelstein received the dubious honor of becoming the third man to lead the Council of Elders. Murmelstein was not new to the Council, and in fact, at one point early on, Commandant Seidl organized the Council with a hierarchy consisting of Epstein at the top, then Edelstein, followed by Murmelstein. With Epstein and Edelstein both dead, Murmelstein seemed the logical choice for Rahm.

It dismayed me that these three dedicated men as well as the rest of the Jewish leadership distrusted each other. I know I have spoken of this before and will no doubt again, but I can't help myself. It's something I feel a constant compulsion to unburden myself of. But with each of these men representing a different faction of European Jewry—Czechoslovakian, German, and Austrian—they seemed destined to view one another with suspicion. The German Authority was aware of this weakness, and they took full advantage of it by disrupting and dividing the Jewish leadership, leaving the Council of Elders plagued by intrigue, suspicion, and mutual recrimination.

From his appearance, one would never think Murmelstein to be such an intelligent man capable of exercising leadership skills. He had a round face and pug nose set atop a fleshy neck and portly body. His small, beady eyes seemed out of proportion amidst his girth, and he spoke with a thick Galician accent. Yet he might well have been the most intelligent of the three Elders or, at least, on par with Herr Doktor Epstein. Murmelstein earned a Doctor of Philosophy and was an ordained rabbi. His phenomenal memory made it impossible to contradict him when he spoke of anything factual—whether something he had read or had been told or had witnessed with his own eyes.

Murmelstein's demeanor contrasted sharply with that of his deputy, Rabbi Leo Baeck, the spiritual leader of German Jewry of whom I will speak later. Baeck had the bearing of Moses, and in many ways, that was how he was perceived—at least by the German Jews. But Baeck's appointment was more honorary and symbolic while Murmelstein labored under intense pressure, as did his two predecessors. Unlike Edelstein and Epstein before him, the German Authority did not get around to killing Murmelstein; he remained at the helm as Elder of the Jews devoting himself selflessly to the task at hand until the day the ghetto was liberated.

CHAPTER FOUR: WAY STATION TO DEATH

Recall I had said that from the day I was conceived by my *paterfamilias*, SS Lieutenant General Reinhard Heydrich, my clandestine mission was to serve as a holding site where Jews who had been collected would be horded like cattle awaiting the slaughterer's blade. And indeed, despite the many deceptive roles I would play during my existence, this was my one and true purpose. The thing is, tens of thousands of Jews died within my walls, and while not anticipated by the men at the Wannsee Conference where I had been born, this surely would have delighted them.

Within my realm, people died in many manners and from various causes. Typhus, along with pneumonia and consumption, killed thousands, especially in my first eighteen months. Soon after I was officially designated a city for elderly German Jews to live out their lives, common ailments associated with old age became the chief cause of death. By December 1943, 28,000 of my residents had succumbed within my so-called protective partitions. In the year and a half leading up to liberation, the daily death rate returned to earlier levels except, ironically enough, at the end when the Germans turned control over to the Red Cross, and typhus ravaged the survivors.

In the beginning, an orderly disposition of the dead was manageable with thirty or so corpses collected every day, but once the daily death rate increased to 100 or more, interring the cadavers became a Herculean task to accomplish with any degree of decorum. Nonetheless, every effort was made to bury the bodies within twenty-four hours in respect for Jewish tradition, although health concerns were also a factor.

The names of the dead and any personal information available were posted at five o'clock each evening. Bodies were transported to the funeral hall where the plain, undecorated coffins were stored. A crew of men was continuously at work constructing the coffins out of rough-hewn planks. A cantor would sing the appropriate prayers in Hebrew, and a rabbi would then read the names of the dead followed by another prayer. Up to twenty-four coffins at a time could be loaded onto the two-tiered carriage that had been painted black and which served as the transport. On the sides of the carriage hung black curtains with bright white Stars of David emblazoned on them.

It wasn't long before the Jewish Administration was compelled to concede that it was unrealistic to expect to be able to dig thousands and thousands of graves. With heavy hearts, heads nodded in agreement that cremation was the only realistic option despite the fact this was inconsistent with the Jewish religion. So instead of wasting labor constructing coffins, the bodies were placed in crude wooden crates with the cremated ashes preserved in numbered cardboard boxes arranged in shelves surrounded by grass and red geraniums in the hope that one day, the remains would be recovered and identified by matching the numbered boxes to the records. But like most aspirations in my domain, this was not to be. In 1944, in stark contrast to the chimneys at Auschwitz spewing flames mixed with Jewish ashes into the black night sky, the Germans ordered that the powdery remains of my people be spilt into the flowing river and left to trickle their way into oblivion.

During my second year, when more than 100 people died every day, men could be seen, their backs stooped and their grunts easily heard, pushing dilapidated two-wheel carts creaking on the cobblestone streets. The pushcarts were filled with the bodies of the dead laid one atop the other, lifeless legs and arms spilling over the sides, the smell of death that announced their arrival lingering long after their departure.

What is less known is that hundreds of my people were out-and-out murdered. Those who violated the rules of the German Authority were imprisoned in the Little Fortress where the despotic SS guards deserved their well-earned reputation for brutality and sadism. Prisoners were tortured, beaten, and killed. A favorite pastime of the SS was to order the inmates to run up steep hills pushing-stone filled wheelbarrows until they collapsed or just dropped dead. Entering the Little Fortress was essentially a death sentence because rarely did anyone emerge alive. Those who did somehow manage to survive inside the Little Fortress were generally used to fill transports heading east where almost everyone was put to death.

Now this may be difficult to comprehend, but because of my ethereal nature, I never slept, so I was aware of everything that went on within me at every moment in time. This was so because as long as even one of my inhabitants had eyes open and did not sleep, which was always the case, I, too, would be awake.

But this is not to say I never suffered from nightmares; indeed, the nightmares of my denizens became my own along with their fears, anxieties, and nocturnal horrors. Such terrors were many and diverse, but everyone, at one time or another, shared the same paramount dread, an angst that can be summed up in one word—a word that was whispered, avoided, and repressed.

When this word was spoken aloud, spreading like a mist and permeating every nook and cranny of my being, everything within me came to a halt; nothing else mattered. The jostling for a better place in the food line ceased; attention drifted so no one could concentrate on their work; people became lackadaisical, and little attention was paid to personal appearances with many who were normally natty becoming slovenly overnight; cultural events and concerts were sparsely attended and held only sporadically; food lacked taste; conversations were clipped; smiles vanished; salutations transformed into curt nods; people were kept at bay; everyone was everyone's enemy because if someone else did not go, then it was all the more likely you would be the one needed to make the quota, to fill the list, to board the dreaded trains heading east to unknown destinations and an unknown fate, though deep down inside, almost everyone feared that one thing and one thing only awaited those on the lurching train cars—death.

Transport. The enunciation of this single word spilling from someone's lips, no matter how offhandedly, brought every man, woman, and child to his or her knees. In everyone's eyes, one could read the dread that might be hidden but not denied: in the wide eyes of the child, the squinty eyes of the former lawyer, the weary eyes of the aged widow, the lusterless eyes of the administrator, the frightened eyes of ... of everyone. The question was always the same. How many are needed this time? Any particular group? Who will be on it? Will my name be on the list? The name of someone I love? How can we avoid it?

When it came to securing protection from transport, most of my people would do almost anything. And who could blame them? They were fighting for their lives. Thus, it was easy to rationalize and justify whatever behavior was required even if it meant relinquishing all rules, laws, and principles of decency. The one objective in everyone's mind was to survive and avoid being placed on the transport list.

For some, the ordeal of awaiting the completion of the transport list was no ordeal at all because they held a designation making them exempt. In the beginning, the 2,500 volunteers who had arrived to construct and establish my physical presence were excused from transport as were up to five persons in each of their families. As I mentioned previously, the prominents were likewise let off as were the members of the Council of Elders along with their families and the Council staff. For most of my existence, the German elderly were spared transport since placing them on the trains traveling east would fly in the face of the charade carefully crafted by the Nazis, that these old Jews would live the remainder of their lives in tranquility within my walls.

I must confess to having reservations about the practice of granting some of my residents exemption from transport, leaving others subject to deportation. The process was, by nature, filled with favoritism. The transport committee was comprised of the Council of Elders and all department heads. Each committee member could submit thirty names to be protected which provided fertile ground for a fierce competition with every member striving to keep their people off the transport lists. Many rationales were argued, such as illness, consideration for past service to the community or in wartime, or working in a vital job. But the truth is that many times these justifications were merely pretenses for personal reasons that could be anything at all.

Those who could not rely on a designation to avoid being placed on the transport list were destined to endure the ordeal which was deliberately designed by the Germans to terrify and create as much anxiety as possible. And the Germans had grown quite adept in satisfying their sadistic streak when it came to making Jews suffer.

Although there were some periods when transports were halted, even during such respites there was always the lingering uneasiness they would resume. However, once a transport was announced, there was no denying that my environs effused sheer terror. Speaking of this raises a very interesting conundrum and one with which I have struggled without ever having reached a satisfactory solution. It is this.

From the most senior members of the Council to the most recent arrival in my realm, most of my Jews seemed to believe the deceitful assurances of the SS that the transports were destined for new Jewish settlements in the east which they would help establish. One might attribute this to wishful thinking, but it had to be more than that, certainly in the face of the growing rumors bolstered by a mounting volume of evidence.

And yet, how could any Jew trust the Germans? How is such a thing possible? To believe the very same people who declared you to be vermin and inhuman creatures suitable for barbaric treatment? To place any credence in the promises that slithered from the twisted lips and perverse sneers of the SS was ludicrous. Indeed, preposterous! Such an inability to acknowledge reality, difficult as it may be, simply eludes me, and I suspect that for most of my people, buried below their consciousness and pressing to burst into the open was the realization of the true destiny awaiting those on the lists for transport.

In any event, on August 24, 1943, no doubt could remain about the fate awaiting those boarding the transports east. The day began much like any other; it was hot and humid with clouds creating a canopy of gray. A group of new arrivals normally would not have drawn anyone's attention, but this group was different: few were over five feet tall; the jittery chatter was high pitched; though frail, their steps still carried a trace of a spring in them as they traipsed the distance to my archways and entered my realm. An entire trainload of children was unheard of and, therefore, a sight to behold by the throngs of my wide-eyed population observing the tramping of little feet over my paved streets.

It wasn't long until the populace spoke of little else, the 1,200 orphaned children from the Bialystok ghetto. They had to be attended to at once, but even before they could be fed, they had to be cleaned, so they were sent to the showers—or, more precisely, one large shower room. As the children warily entered the chamber and realized where they were, their weary but friendly faces contorted into masks of fear; the lips that had formed slight smiles blew apart with mouths open wide, and a mammoth wailing swelled like a surging tsunami pounding everything in its wake. The cries reverberated from the walls and into the halls and outside the doors, flooding my domain; not a single set of ears could avoid the bone-chilling screams. A more gruesome sound I had never heard, and it will haunt me forever.

It was only after great effort and assurances that they merely had to be cleansed before being fed that the children calmed down. It turned out that the source of their panic was the stories they had heard about what awaited those Jews traversing the rails once they reached the end of the line; of how, when arriving at their destination, they were directed to shower rooms; that where instead of water spilling from the shower heads, gas spewed forth, filling the room; and how, in the end, after their listless, naked bodies were pulled and tugged and dragged to the ovens, the Jews departed as ashes flaring up the chimney into the coal-black sky. From the mouths of children. How could any doubt remain? How could such a scenario be anything but true?

Perhaps it was out of a sense of helplessness in the face of the German edict demanding names to fill the slots of the death trains mixed with a desire to exert some control over their lives that my denizens developed a strict protocol. Orderliness in the midst of calamity can provide a small measure of comfort and no more so than for my German Jews who had once lived in an exact and stringent culture. Sometimes the procedure varied, but it always began with the issuance of a directive from the Germans to prepare a list of a specific number of names of at least 1,000. Normally, there would be a period of three days from receipt of the German order to the day of transport, which for some, quite literally, was a lifetime.

With the order in hand and the number of slots to be filled, the committee retired to a conference room. In the center of the large table was a current list of all the names of my inhabitants. From this list, names would be culled to fill the transport. Shoulders slouched, jackets off, sleeves rolled up, pitchers of water filled, ersatz coffee flowing into cups, the committee members prepared to do their work, which they knew would still be going on with the break of dawn the next day. Sometimes shouting could be heard through the closed door, but mostly, the voices were muted, the tones weary and inflections resigned. People quibbled, questioned, considered, contested, and most of all, bargained with each other as they deliberated. In the end, the list was complete, and a notice of the first assignment was made available to my population.

The most common two words spoken within minutes from distribution of the list of first assignment were "in it." Are you "in it?" Is your husband "in it?" How about Frau Goldenfarb? I hear she and her family are "in it." Are my children "in it?" Am I "in it?" Necks craned, eyes squinted, heads weaved and bobbed above shoulders or thrusted through the spaces between the skulls blocking the view of the notices containing the names of those assigned for transport posted on the walls. Being "in it" was mostly met with resignation; occasionally, a few people, when spotting their names, were pleased, especially if they had been my residents for some time and were sick of my milieu and indulged themselves in the fantasy that the transports were headed east to establish new and better living quarters.

But others could be seen bustling down my streets and darting through alleys, taking steps two at a time, running in corridors to secure an appointment with someone who would hear their case for exemption. Arguments were based on the usual grounds, such as family needs and maintaining families as a unit, especially parents with young children. When it became impossible to allow parents and children to remain together, the policy shifted with families transported intact. Single people had little chance of being removed. Not-so-honorable acts of bribery were stealthily made to be taken off the list, proffering cigarettes, extra food rations, clothing, and even promises for rewards once the War was at an end.

One might think that not seeing one's name on the notice of first assignment would be greeted with a sigh of relief, but everyone knew some names would be removed which meant other names had to be added as replacements. The numbers must be filled one way or the other, and for the most part, the Germans didn't care who was bound for transport. However, there were occasions when the sadistic nature of the Nazi beast could not resist even this aspect of their rule. Once, Commandant Seidl ordered all 250 women from one barracks to be included for transport because they heated a room without permission. Following this, to torment Edelstein, he ordered the Elder to select two of the women to be removed thus forcing Edelstein to decide which two particular women would be spared.

Once the final list was complete, a summons was issued for each person to be transported. The small, two-centimeter-wide strip of colored paper was accompanied by a sheet of detailed instructions including what one was allowed to take. The best time to deliver the summons was when nearly everyone could be found in their assigned place—at night, where they slept, although few managed to sleep on the nights when the notices were delivered by the ghetto police to the house elders. Like specters gliding through a darkened sky, the house elders could be seen slipping between the beddings of the inmates, passing out the unwanted information.

Once the summons were delivered, appeals were rarely successful. This, in turn, invited desperation which ultimately bred panic. Hence, it was inevitable that early the next morning, hundreds of sleep-deprived and frightened people would storm the offices of the Council of Elders, crashing into one another, screaming and shouting and demanding an appointment with someone, anyone, of authority. But as I said, for the most part, their fate was sealed, and within hours, an eerie silence would prevail, and one by one, the unfortunates shuffled off.

Those summoned were normally told to assemble at a specific location, usually a courtyard, where they would remain for one or two days sleeping on straw sacks. Their luggage and other belongings were placed in piles. Every effort was made to alleviate the distress; food was plentiful, and if someone lacked clothing or shoes or a blanket, a replacement would be supplied. But no matter the efforts to assuage these poor souls, sorrow, anxiety, and outright fear permeated the air. It was all too evident in the mournful eyes, sagging faces, dragging feet, uneaten meals, and the way a mother gazed upon her child when she thought no one was looking.

When the train was ready to depart, the people were instructed to retrieve their belongings and make the march to the Bauschowitz station. In almost no time, everyone was gone, and the courtyard was empty like a ghost town; home, now, only to the phantasms of its previous occupants and awaiting the next batch of forlorn souls.

Walking four and five abreast and guarded by Czech police accoutered in long drab coats, the Jews tramped through the town of Bauschowitz heading toward the train station. Slogging along, my former inmates carried their small suitcases with their other belongings often slung over their shoulders. Even on warm days, the Jews wore several layers of clothing and in winter as many coats as they could muster. Standing off to the side as the parade passed by, the townsfolk, mostly women wearing long-sleeved dresses and aprons taking a break from their household chores, stood in small groups making idle conversation, paying no attention to the stick-like figures clopping along the cobbled streets on their way to the station. My people were ignored as if they did not exist; and for most, in a matter of days, that would be the case.

Such scenes were repeated many times beginning with the very first transport on January 9, 1942, an unusually frigid day even for my environment. The temperature was well below zero, and frost was hanging in the air, attaching itself like a parasite to the exposed faces of my residents. Just before sunrise, the first transport, marked O, creaked over the tracks heading eastward for Riga. Six days after that, another transport, marked P, departed from the station. There would be many others to follow—sixty to be exact—carrying 87,000 of my denizens to places of mass extermination or, if they were fortunate, to concentration camps. Of these 87,000, less than 4,000 survived.

During that first year, most of the 42,000 selected for twenty-three transports were Czech Jews of which only 224 survived. As I have said, old German and Austrian Jews were exempt to facilitate the façade that I was a haven for the Reich's elderly Jews, but later on, this would give way to more practical considerations as the old became a burden, and they eventually became prime candidates for the list.

It was a macabre sight to behold when in the fall of 1942, some of the German elderly were selected for transport to decrease my population. Ill, feeble, alarmed, bewildered, alone, helpless—faces pleading for some explanation, assistance, even a quick end—the old people dragged themselves to the train station; some were even sitting on hearses being pushed through my deserted streets in the pre-dawn hours while everyone else slept, or pretended to. Their destination was Auschwitz/Birkenau, a place unheard of until then, and they marked the first transport directly sent to the infamous killing complex of four gas chambers exterminating 6,000 Jews daily.

However, the elderly German and Austrian inmates received a reprieve a few months later when Heydrich's successor, Ernst Kaltenbrunner, petitioned Himmler for permission to transport more of these old Jews who could not hold down any jobs contributing to the War effort and were therefore expendable. But Himmler turned down this request to maintain the pretense that I was indeed a lovely city for the elderly Germanic Jews to live out the remainder of their lives in tranquility. Ultimately, everyone received a respite in February of 1943 when a transport of 1,000 inmates became the last to depart for six months.

A short time later, in April, my demographics became even more diverse; the first group of Jews from Holland arrived. Unlike the majority of their compatriots who were sent to the Westerbork transit camp and then shipped to Auschwitz, these Jews making the march from the Bauschowitz station to my fortress gates were considered privileged for one reason or another. I marveled at how normal the Dutch Jews appeared arriving in ordinary passenger trains, the men accoutered in pressed suits and starched shirts, the women adorned in fancy dresses as if going to dinner and the theater. Many had packed butter and chocolates in their suitcases just in case there would be some shortage of these culinary delights in the fine cuisine they expected was awaiting them.

These Jews hadn't a clue, totally unsuspecting like innocents being led to the slaughter. Not even when tramping over my streets did they possess even an inkling of where they really were and what their remaining days would be like. Not until amassed at the intake station, pushed and shoved, shouted at, searched, suitcases torn from their grips, husbands and wives separated, crying children wrenched from their parents' arms … and then assigned to their quarters: wooden bunks, outhouses. Only then did their smug and carefree faces give way to bewilderment, furrowed foreheads, backs stiffened in indignation, shouts of anger, teary eyes, quivering lips, clenched jaws stifling cries, and finally, blank stares and sunken shoulders slowly surrendering to their new reality.

My population was also increased at that time with 500 Jews from Denmark who had it remarkably well because their conditions were monitored by the Danish Red Cross which, unlike the International or German Red Cross, took an active interest to see their charges were treated humanely. So from the very beginning, the Danish Jews were treated differently, receiving a special welcome from Commandant Burger, SS officials, and Epstein and then assigned to the barracks previously occupied by the Bialystok ghetto's children. All of these Danish Jews were afforded special privileges: they could write letters more often, receive parcels from home, and most important, under special orders from Eichmann himself, they were exempt from transport. I often wondered how different things might have been if the International Red Cross expressed a similar degree of concern for those dependent upon them, but I'll get to this later when I speak of the official Red Cross visit, a very disheartening affair indeed.

Unfortunately, the respite from transports did not last long. The summer of 1943 was insufferably hot. The heat, accentuated by the unbearable overcrowding, made it difficult to even breathe, let alone sleep. And the merciless onslaught of bugs and fleas did not help. Sleeping in the rooms and barracks became impossible for many, and as the hours dragged from evening into night, people lifted themselves from their bedding and trudged into the halls and outdoors seeking a spot where they could at least sit, if not lie down and surrender to a state of semi-slumber.

It was during this summer that my domain felt the effects of the Jewish resistance fighters in the Warsaw ghetto who had made their gallant uprising against the might of the German Army that spring. The Germans had not only been embarrassed and furious, they grew fearful that similar revolts would take place in other ghettos and camps, and they became increasingly apprehensive about the younger Jews inhabiting such places. Since the Czech Jewish population was comprised of people of all ages, the decision was made to rid my domain of all the young and able-bodied Czech Jews.

On September 6, 1943, 5,000 Protectorate Jews of working age and their families were deported east and a special family camp was established in Auschwitz/Birkenau to receive these deportees. Leo Janowitz, the general secretary of the Council of Elders and Edelstein's right-hand man, was given the questionable honor of being in charge to administer this new facility. But before the Council would agree to implement this plan, they demanded assurances that this new facility was similar to my domain. Upon receiving word from the World Jewish Congress that the International Red Cross obtained confirmation that this was, indeed, a new facility modeled after me, Janowitz and others set off with hopes to establish an independent community for Jews to reside in relative peace.

Needless to say, this was not so. The Germans were successful in convincing the Red Cross, never a difficult task, that Birkenau was a large camp comprised of Birkenau and several other towns in Upper Silesia separate and distinct from the Auschwitz camp where conditions were believed to be harsh. In this new community with a population of 35,000, the people would work in mines, metal industries, and the manufacture of synthetic rubber. In fact, Birkenau was a sub-camp of Auschwitz, and instead of serving as a model city where Jews could work and live as Janowitz and others had anticipated, it became a model extermination facility in the mass murder of Jews.

The special family camp in Birkenau for my people was established to facilitate this charade. Most importantly, my former residents were spared the selection process, and in addition, they were entitled to wear their own clothes and were not assigned to the slave labor squads. The Nazi guards strutted among them distributing postcards, gently commanding them to write to relatives giving assurances that they had arrived safely and were well. "You do not want your family and friends to needlessly worry about you, do you?" They would ask with a patronizing smile.

Once the postdated cards were collected, the new arrivals no longer served any purpose, and most were promptly dispatched to the gas chambers. The postcards were mailed to promote the hope among my people that the transports to Birkenau did not mean a death sentence but only, as the German Authority had pronounced, a relocation. Ironically, sometimes the postcards arrived after the scriveners had become ashes disgorged from the crematoria chimneys.

The transports continued with seven more carrying 19,517 of my residents to Auschwitz/Birkenau through May 1944. There was a lull in transports because of the Red Cross visit, but they resumed on September 28, 1944, with eleven transports dispatching 18,402 Jews to Auschwitz/Birkenau in one month alone. Of these Jews, 1,574 survived.

In early October 1944, notices were posted that shook the inmates over sixty from their sense of complacency. In a few lines, the populace was informed that everyone up to the age of sixty-five was to prepare for transport and be ready for call-up on the nights of Saturday, October 8 and Sunday, October 9. Now, only the very old would remain along with those possessing designations exempting them from transport. It was like a bolt of lightning striking out of a clear, cerulean sky. Once again, my relatively organized world converted into one of chaos with people scrambling, pleading, imploring, shouting, doing anything and everything to gain an audience with someone of authority—up to and including Dr. Murmelstein and members of the Council—in a desperate attempt to have their names deleted from the call-up list that was to total 6,000 inmates.

As promised, the call-ups began on Saturday evening with scores of house elders reading names from lists; 2,700 inmates lifted their luggage and carried their belongings, shuffling along the darkened streets to the barracks where they would wait for the next step. Few slept that night, and there was a constant undercurrent of murmurings with people rehearsing what they would say to an official before boarding the train in the hope they might secure a last-minute reprieve.

The next day, at five o'clock a.m., orders were issued to prepare for boarding. It was a warm day for October. Teams of helpers in white caps aided the elderly with their belongings. Observing the old folks schlep their stuffed and frayed baggage, Philipp Manes thought to himself how generous the German Authority was to allow the people to take so many personal effects with them. It was at that moment that I finally lost my patience with Manes and those like him who, despite the suffering and treatment they received at the hands of the Germans, still remained devoted to the *Vaterland*. "Blind fools!" I wanted to scream, but despite my omniscience, I had no direct way to communicate with those who composed my corpus like so many tiny, quivering cells oblivious to my existence.

The procedure began with the announcement of those to depart first. As names were called, people bid their farewells, some forcing smiles while others avoided eye contact at all costs. Two hours later, 1,600 people from the first group of 2,700 were loaded on the transport with many still believing that the destination was a labor camp where they could continue to work for the War effort. Those remaining had an extra day to prepare themselves for the next transport: to put their affairs in order and bid their good-byes. For most staying behind like Manes, it was difficult saying farewell to those departing since many were convinced it was not likely they would ever see each other again. But this was not because they had entertained the possibility they would be murdered; rather, they feared that after the War they would never see their homeland again, leaving them scattered to the four corners of the earth, wandering Jews homeless once more.

These old German Jews continued to mull about as though they were boarding a train to take them to some esoteric vacation spot, comporting themselves with the decorum of which they were well known. Scenes of formal farewells repeated themselves throughout the day. Dr. Martin Kraemer approached Manes to make his good-bye with his wife, Valerie, the Duchess of Alencon, standing stiffly by his side. Kraemer's stately demeanor befitted his doctorate of law and military experience as a cavalry captain, but beneath it dwelled an imaginative personality capable of composing epic poems, which he delivered in public readings during the time he spent with me.

Not far off, Rabbi Regina Jonas stood stiffly with her shoulders squared, projecting a formidable persona. A woman of forty-two, she had been restricted to conducting services in Germany to the outlying communities because she had not been recognized by the more urbane and pious among the Jewish religious establishment to officiate anywhere else. In my realm, the good Rabbi was likewise looked down upon and left to perform pastoral duties, which given the conditions, were many indeed. Rabbi Regina could have remained but elected instead to accompany her mother to whatever destination awaited them. The two women waited hand in hand to board the train.

Waving to Manes from a window in the transport as the train began to pull out was Melly Weiss, an opera soubrette and singer who, at one time, performed all over Europe and could speak and sing in seven languages. She was a vibrant and confidant woman, but as she faded from Manes's view, her face formed an unfamiliar expression of doubt and despair.

There was a temporary lull in further transports, providing time for rumors to circulate.

"Did you hear the age is to be raised to seventy on the next transport?" someone clearly not seventy would ask.

"No," a man might respond, "What would they possibly want with me? I'm too old to be relocated. It would be more trouble than it is worth. What kind of work can I do that could benefit the War effort?"

But the seed had been planted, and like a stubborn weed, it would grow and take hold, soon overcoming much of the populace. The days became interminable with little to do but wait.

Transports resumed on October 14, another warm and sunny day. The group selected for that transport included many who were sick and immobile, although there were more than a few like Trude Pick, the pretty and youthful director of the allowances department, who had volunteered for the transport to be with an old and infirm parent. Such acts of devotion were not uncommon. Sometimes loved ones fought over whether they should leave together or have one remain behind. Willi Durra, who conducted the choir while a resident of mine, firmly insisted that his young wife, an efficient draftswoman and excellent caricaturist, remain while he departed. If he was forced, he told her with a glare that said he meant every word, he'd bind her with ropes to keep her from joining him. Despite the glint of a tear in his eye, the stern gaze prevailed, and Durra's wife remained.

More transports followed. Some people panicked and hid themselves after seeing their names posted on the list. But this rarely spared them, and eventually they would be found, rounded up, and taken into detention. Others radiated an air of stoicism and dignity. Jakob Wolffing, formerly an attorney who had served as a member of the Council of Elders and head of the finance department, boarded the train looking like a Greek scholar with his rosy, fresh complexion and snow-white hair. Others displayed acts of selflessness like Dr. Ernst Podvinec who, not wishing to leave anything behind, distributed the vegetables and tomatoes he grew in his garden. His heart ached as he envisaged the youngsters he cared for in the children's home whom he was now forced to abandon.

On October 28, 1944, the last transport departed from the Bauschowitz station destined for Auschwitz. The 2,038 inmates who had been selected were assigned in groups of fifty or more to fill cattle trucks. Seventeen-year-old Alice Ehrmann shuddered as the last tiny hatches were nailed shut with metal plates. The people inside crouched on the baggage heaps in utter blackness, struggling to breath the closed, dank air for the next twenty-four hours. Upon their arrival in Auschwitz, the Jews from the final transport leaving my domain had the dubious distinction of also being the last batch of Jews to fill the gas chambers of Birkenau. The day after their arrival at Auschwitz, Himmler ordered the gas facilities to cease operations.

After October 28, I became unrecognizable. My streets no longer were teeming with people scurrying to and fro. In fact, so many of my residents were over sixty-five that the steps echoing on the streets and sidewalks crept along so slowly, they sounded more like a light drizzle than a steady shower. Without a workforce, the offices became quiet. With so many gone, there was little to administer, and of what purpose was a self-administering city as Edelstein had once envisioned if there was nothing to administer?

There was an eerie silence, as well—a quiet that had once been so fervently sought and dreamt of now hung in the air like a heavy mist after a storm, a stark reminder that one should be careful for what one wishes. Silence was felt in another quarter, as well. With the musicians and singers gone, there were no more performances; no music was played; no operettas were sung. Shadows became visible in hallways; previously concealed corners now exposed themselves in the barracks; alleyways were accessible for privacy, but suddenly, few sought seclusion. Solitude was readily available, but who desired it? One could only muse over the missing faces of acquaintances, friends, and loved ones. Only 11,000 Jews remained including 819 children at the expiration of this final series of transports.

But more Jews would arrive and in ways least expected.

CHAPTER FIVE: THE COMMANDANTS

Returning to a time before I made my first appearance, the last part of November 1941 and only two months after my conception, the first advance unit of Czech Jews, known as the A-K in ghetto speak, arrived at the town Theresienstadt to begin preparations for the transformation from a garrison-town to a concentration camp. Although the German soldiers who had occupied the military barracks had departed, many of the Czech civilians remained in their homes; children were still traipsing off in the early morning hours clutching school bags and lunch packages; shopkeepers raised the blinds and unlocked their doors eagerly awaiting their first customers; women strung wash to dry on the clotheslines in their backyards, dallying amongst themselves and gossiping about the strange new arrivals, all of whom were men and mostly young. From the word going around, these men were all Jews kept busy at work cleaning and repairing the barracks the Germans had so hastily vacated.

On an especially cold December morning, the already haggard and malnourished Jewish men gathered to be addressed by Richard Skarabis, the temporary commandant. Skarabis had cut his teeth in the infamous Łódź ghetto in Poland, which was the first ghetto the Germans purposely and methodically established for the Jews. At one time, the ghetto was inhabited by almost a quarter million residents before it was liquidated, dispatching those still alive to killing and labor camps. Skarabis knew the score. At Łódź, there had also been a Council of Elders, but as would be the case in my domain, the real power and authority lay with the Germans.

In keeping with his position, Skarabis held himself erect, glaring at the motley throng before him. Though dawn was barely breaking, the men appeared weary; their shoulders tilted, and they kept shifting from one foot to the other to avoid freezing in place. Skarabis demanded their attention and addressed the group, setting the tone for what was to be their future and the nature of my being.

"Today we're on top," Skarabis proclaimed, referring to the Germans, his lips twisting into a scornful sneer. "Tomorrow," he shouted, "you're on the bottom!"

The Jewish men gazed at one another in bewilderment, not knowing what he was talking about. But as the days and weeks turned into months and years, no words would ever ring truer, and there would not be a resident of mine who would ever doubt what Skarabis had ordained that day. Such was the pecking order in my domain with the man at the pinnacle being the camp's commandant of whom there were three. The first, Siegfried Seidl, assumed command in December 1941, and he had the longest tenure, which did not end until June 1943.

Like many of those who carried out the Nazi agenda, Seidl was not only an ardent and dedicated Nazi but also well educated. An Austrian, he held a doctorate from the University of Vienna in history and German studies. By the time he was appointed commandant of Theresienstadt, Seidl had been a member of the Austrian National Socialist Party for more than a decade, having joined when he was nineteen. Indeed, his wife, a former kindergarten teacher who was also a member of the Party and a supporting member of the SS even before they married, shared his political views. At the age of thirty, Seidl was on the ascent with a long and promising career before him. Young, committed, and intelligent, he seemed the perfect choice to transform the German garrison into a model city to function as a showplace for the world to see just how well the Jews fared under the benign Nazi regime—or at least that was the opinion held by Eichmann who, along with Heydrich, my *paterfamilias*, signed Seidl's appointment.

Though young, Seidl had attained the rank of *SS Obersturmführer*. While in my realm, he would be promoted once again to the rank of *SS Hauptsturmführer*. He had already proven himself when he had arranged for the efficient transport of Jews from Wartegau to Poland in 1939. Because of his ability to understand what it takes to control large numbers of Jews, he did not hesitate to voice his opposition to the plan that 80,000 of the parasitic race could be concentrated in the ghetto when he believed no more than 30,000 could be properly confined. Nonetheless, he was overruled but only for a time; it was not long before he eventually obtained the numbers he desired through executions, beatings, disease, and transports to the killing camps.

Because he was an intelligent and educated man, Seidl tacked a different course in communicating with his subjects than the approach taken by Skarabis in his infamous speech to the first Jewish arrivals. He conveyed his message in a more understated manner but no less convincing. Upon entering his office, one could not help but notice the figurine prominently positioned on his desk, least of all Jakob Edelstein who frequented Seidl's office on a daily basis to receive the Orders of the Day and make whatever supplications he felt he stood a chance of petitioning without being summarily dismissed. The figure was a caricature of a Jew with the inscription, "Don't get angry, always smile." And, indeed, this became the decorum Jews adopted in their few direct dealings with the Germans, from Edelstein to the other members of the Council to the staff and to all my denizens, though rarely, if ever, did the ordinary resident find an occasion to address a German.

Despite the servile smile that manifested itself on Edelstein's face whenever he entered Seidl's quarters and for that matter, similar smiling visages presenting themselves whenever the commandant had the misfortune to come close to a Jewish inmate, this did little to assuage Seidl's sadistic streak, which brewed like lava flowing beneath the surface ready to erupt without a moment's notice. Some satisfy ruthless tendencies in subtle ways, which is what I would have expected from a man like Seidl, an Austrian with a doctorate degree; but in practice, the commandant preferred the direct and cold-blooded approach. Though tens of thousands died within my walls from disease, starvation, and physical deprivations, this was not enough for Seidl who demanded more Jewish lives, which he accomplished by directing beatings of the inmates and even ordering executions, a practice that ceased with his departure.

Perhaps had he not been so brutal and obvious, he might have been the only commandant I would have known. But because he was not in sufficient sympathy with my purpose as envisioned by Heydrich and Eichmann, to be an archetypal ghetto for old people, Seidl was relieved of his duties and dispatched to service where his voracious appetite for inflicting pain, punishment, and death could be put to better use—commandant at Bergen-Belsen.

If the Germans removed Seidl because he was the wrong person to promote my image that I was a place of decorum and comfort for elderly Germans of the Hebrew faith to live the remainder of their lives in tranquility, substituting him with

Anton Burger as the new commandant confounds all reason and makes me wonder what Eichmann could possibly have been thinking. How could such a virulent anti-Semite be constitutionally capable of carrying out the pretext Eichmann and Heydrich so eagerly desired? Even among the Nazis and their collaborators, Burger stood out as a particularly pernicious Jew-hater.

The man was fanatical in his anti-Semitism. So fervent was his racism that whenever he was in the offices of the Jewish Council or staff, he opened the door with his elbow so he would not dirty his hands with "Jewish emanations." One of his first orders was self-defeating: forbidding the SS to use Jewish doctors or domestics, as had long been common under Seidl. And because his loathing toward Czechs was almost on par with his hatred of Jews, the Jews of the Protectorate, both Jewish and Czecho-slovakian, which, at the time, composed most of my residents and leadership, proved an especially desirable target for his fury.

When the Council of Elders learned that Seidl had been replaced with the Austrian Anton Burger, a chill cut through the air.

"A bad omen," someone said, and others nodded, taking note that he was being transferred from Auschwitz about which rumors abounded, none of them benign. Almost everyone in the room knew of Burger. It was said he had eyes so cold that his stare could render a person immobile if struck by its glare. He was a gigantic man whose physical presence was intimidating like that of a snorting bull stirring up dust in a rage. He was a veteran SS man to the core, having worked his way up the ranks to *Sturmbannführer*, earning a reputation for efficiently evacuating Belgian, Dutch, and French Jews.

Burger was also known to most of the Council for the time he had spent in Prague. Stories abounded. Once when a Jew had been assured of immigration to America after paying all the fees and bribes that were demanded, Burger intervened at the last minute, extorting additional payments with the gusto of a guest arriving late for dinner and gorging himself on the final remains.

Another incident was even better known to the members of the Council since it directly involved their leader. One time back in Prague, Burger had been asked by his superiors to deliver a speech to the SS about the German orders of knighthood. In a panic, not having any knowledge on the subject and given his lack of education, he did not even know where to begin to gather the information. But greater than his ignorance was his vanity, so rather than seek the aid of a fellow German officer, he sought out a

Jew. After all, he must have considered, despite their vile nature, they were known to be smart, and by picking a Jew, he could be assured the secret would remain safe. He'd make certain the Yid understood what would happen if word ever got out. The death would be a slow and torturous one and not just for the Yid alone but his entire family as well. Ironically, the man he selected to write the lecture was Jakob Edelstein whom fate would bring once more within his sphere in my domain.

Before entering the SS, Burger, the son of a stationery dealer, had been an elementary school teacher. While I imagine he relished this role, it was likely not for the purpose of infusing young minds with knowledge. Nor can I envision him rustling the hair of a young boy nor tweaking the cheek of a little girl nor providing an encouraging pat on the shoulder while a student struggled with a problem.

What I visualize when I think of Burger the school teacher is a bully; a stern, unsmiling man, only half educated and arrogant, holding little tolerance for the slightest deviation from the decorum he exacted in his classroom and demanding respect be paid him at every opportunity. More likely than not, corporeal punishment was his first and only resort as a pedagogy over reason and compassion.

Of even greater concern to the Council was Burger's reputation as a man who was actually fond of violence. All of which, coupled with the fact he was believed to be an imbecile, terrified the Jews who had to deal with him. Indeed, their fears turned out to be justified.

A fanatic for lists and charts, Burger ordered the infamous census of November 1943 whereby the entire Jewish population stood in place for almost a full day in the frigid, damp air, leaving corpses strewn on the ground like fallen limbs from the trees. On another occasion, Burger ordered all A-K members, who, until then, had been exempt from transport, to be examined. Those with soft hands were placed on the transport list since clearly they had not been engaged in physical labor.

After eight months, it was clear to the Germans that once again they had made a mistake. Though Burger had begun preparations for my face-lift in anticipation of the Red Cross Visit, he was simply neither the man for the job nor the visage to be presented to the world to prove how well my Jews were being treated by the benevolent German Authority. In February 1944, the third and last commandant assumed his position within my realm.

In keeping with what had become a tradition in selecting my commandants, the Germans once again settled upon an Austrian, knowing their anti-Semitism was homegrown and not foisted upon them. This is not to say that Germany was not rife with anti-Semitism but only that some joined the Party out of practical concerns perhaps to advance a career or even retain a position. But those Austrians who had aligned themselves with the Nazi Party long before the *Anschluss* were Jew-haters through and through. All that varied were the faces they wore as they helped pave the way for unification with Germany and the establishment of Nazi rule.

Such a man was Karl Rahm who was thirty-seven when he became commandant. In his former life, while apprenticing as a toolmaker in Vienna, he was exposed to the activities of the Austrian Nazi Party and became a member in the early 1930s while also joining the underground of the Austrian SS.

SS Captain Karl Rahm assumed command in February 1944 and remained until May 1945, scurrying away like a wounded wolf just before liberation. Prior to arriving in my dominion, he had served under Eichmann, and then when transferred to Prague, he became a close associate of Hans Günther, the Director of the Central Office for the Solution of the Jewish Problem in the Protectorate. Working in that job, he learned the importance of language and the way words could be manipulated and plied to deceive and misinform, a skill that was essential in creating the illusion that I would portray before an all too receptive worldwide audience.

Where Seidl had been wily like a fox in his treatment of the Jews, and Burger behaved more like a voracious lion with an insatiable appetite for Jewish flesh, Rahm projected an urbane and pleasant public persona belying a heinous viciousness. When Dr. Paul Epstein, the new head of the Council of Elders following the arrest of Edelstein, first met the new commandant, he took the man in. The countenance was innocuous enough, he must have considered, observing the oblong face, full forehead, dark, wavy hair brushed back, deep-set eyes, and lips sealed shut unless he was speaking. Rahm sat stiffly with excellent posture while Epstein pondered how Burger's replacement could have been a lot worse since this man was probably more like a dog who barks rather than bites. Indeed, Rahm did establish an interesting, almost cordial relationship with some of my denizens, especially those who shared his working-class background, and for a bribe, he could even be induced to keep someone off the transport list. But Epstein only saw a luminous disposition and not the dark side of the lunar-like visage.

Rahm was a product of the Austrian middle class, an important consideration given the task he was expected to accomplish—supervising my transformation before the Red Cross visit. A mechanic by profession, he immersed himself in the details of constructing facades to fool the Red Cross delegation, which turned out not to be a difficult undertaking either because of their gullibility or their desire to remain ignorant of the truth ... but more of this later.

Rahm went about his assignment the way he would rebuild an old and over-worked engine, transforming it into an efficient and reliable machine. He valued the importance of each part running in sync with the others, knowing that just as a failure of a pin or bolt in a motor would spell the stopping of the engine, every man, woman, and child; every false wall, temporary garden, open pavilion; every dining room table with a spread of delicacies for the population must operate in cohesion in order to convince the world just how wonderful a realm I had become for my Jews.

Like the variegated flower gardens grown for the occasion of the Red Cross visit, Rahm gloried in the beautification program. As it evolved and progress was made, the third commandant's face actually beamed, eyes glowed in the pride he took with his accomplishment. Indeed in the minds of some of the populace, he even was considered a receptive gentleman.

But make no mistake. Like his predecessors, the man was a murderer efficient and effective in dispatching tens of thousands of men, women, and children to their deaths. In some ways, Rahm was the worst of the bunch because just like the false veneer he offered to the world concealing the ugly truth of my true nature, in a similar fashion he presented his own visage—polite, smiling, and gracious—while secreting from sight his splotched hands stained with the blood that had spurted from the veins of people he considered no more than vermin. Rahm was a cynic as well as rash, a dangerous combination; easily incited to anger, he never hesitated to beat an inmate, which he did frequently, or to personally oversee torture sessions. But unlike Burger, he successfully concealed this aspect of his personality from the public eye.

Eventually, however, Rahm was unable to maintain the innocent pretense he had skillfully fashioned. Once the War was over, the Czech authorities prose-cuted several members of the SS including Rahm and Seidl. The first and last of my commandants were tried, convicted, sentenced to death, and executed. Ironically, Anton Burger, the most brutal of the three, escaped the Czech clutches. Tried in abstentia, he was sentenced to death, as well, but the sentence was never carried out. Despite the fact he had been arrested twice, he escaped both times and in 1951, disap-peared without a trace. Settling in Eisen, West Germany under an assumed identity,

Burger led a quiet life until his death in 1991. It wasn't until three years later that his identity was uncovered. I seriously doubt the man held even an ounce of remorse for what he had done.

CHAPTER SIX: THE GERMAN JEWS ARRIVE

The first German Jews to enter my domain in May 1942 were happenstance. In keeping with the policy of Joseph Goebbels, always the master of propaganda, an exhibit had been constructed in the homeland called the Soviet Paradise which was designed to depict the low standard of living of the Russians, Germany's one-time ally-turned-foe. A fire had broken out at the exhibit which was determined to be arson, and the blame was put at the hands of five Jews. As a result, 500 German Jews were arrested; the men were either shot or dispatched to concentration camps. Not knowing what to do with their wives and children, it was decided to send them to me.

But it was really not until the summer of 1942 that SS Lieutenant General Reinhard Heydrich's vision for what I was to be became a reality with the arrival of a transport from Germany on June 2 consisting of fifty Jews from Berlin. Two and a half weeks later, almost 1,000 Austrian Jews arrived from Vienna. Ultimately, 42,000 Jews from Germany, 15,000 Austrian Jews, and another 1,000 Jews from other parts of the Greater German Reich became my reluctant denizens.

If my entire existence was nothing but a charade—a sham the Germans set forth before an all too receptive worldwide audience—nowhere was it more evident than in the expressions of the wizened visages of those former German citizens of the Hebrew faith as they alighted from the trains in Bauschowitz.

I saw it in their upturned faces eagerly seeking a welcoming environment, eyes betraying a glimmer of hope as they walked with a briskness belying their advanced years. Their belief that the fatherland remained their country and had only been temporarily abducted by the Nazis made them susceptible to the carefully laid pretense that this move was not deportation but only a relocation. After all, they surmised, why else would the lists delineating what to bring be so explicit: bedroll and blankets; shirts, slacks, shoes, and underwear; sweaters and coats; pots, bowls, tea strainers, forks, and spoons. Clearly, their accommodations would be satisfactory though not what they had been accustomed to, they thought.

Of course, it did not take long for the wall of this façade to crumble, albeit gradually, in bits and pieces. But it did fall apart except to the most gullible and blind of these Jews of the Reich, Jews like Herr Doktor Carl von Weinberg and Philipp Manes. Von Weinberg had been a powerful man in Germany as deputy chairman of the consulting board of IG Farben. When the Nazis came to power in 1933, he was convinced he was impervious from persecution, confiding to a DuPont official, "Although I am a Jew, I've given the Nazi movement my full stamp of approval!" And yet, at the age of eighty-one, he found himself shipped to my domain, and the white-haired man with small features sadly had to admit that the oversized decorations glittering in his lapel did him little good as he lay dying in the arms of a stranger, a gray-haired woman named Mrs. Martha Klein von Peci who nursed him in his terminal illness.

Manes was less distinguished than many, yet he contributed more than most to improve the life in my milieu. A former fur merchant from Berlin, Manes organized more than 500 cultural events before he and his wife were transported to Auschwitz. A thoroughly assimilated Jew, he retained both his Jewish and German identity, and he remained a patriotic German to the end, deeming it an honor to labor on behalf of the War effort for the homeland. Indeed, when he tried to imagine the damage from Allied air bombardments raining down upon his beloved Munich, it left him heartbroken. Manes rationalized the treatment he received under the Third Reich by comparing the regime to parents who should be honored and respected by their children even when chastising their wayward offspring. "Why should our attitude toward the fatherland be different?" he would ask. Why, the man was even grateful to the German authorities for their humane treatment and justified the lethal transports as necessary so the Germans could regulate the ghetto.

Even as the last transport pulled away from the Bauschowitz station with Manes and his wife, Gertrude, as passengers, he considered how generous and tolerant the German authorities had been during his two-year stay with me. Of course, whether he still harbored such feelings when he faced execution in Auschwitz, I have no way of knowing, though it would not have surprised me if he did. After all, many of these Jews had their familial roots embedded in Germany for centuries, and they had prospered in business and joined the professional ranks. For the most part, society was open to them as they assimilated into the larger gentile community. Nonetheless, following a decade of Nazi rule, Manes and von Weinberg, with their steadfast allegiance to the fatherland, found themselves in the minority, and most of my German Jews, at least those with their eyes and minds still open, learned of my true nature soon enough.

Such was the state of affairs late in the afternoon of September 10, 1942 with the arrival of a fresh transport. When the train pulled into the station at Bauschowitz, an eerie quiet greeted the rolling rail cars as they screeched to a halt on the rusted tracks. Suddenly, the stillness that had permeated the small depot was shattered by shouts of "Schnell! Macht Schnell!" barked by German soldiers strutting like warlords in their drab gray coats. Czech police in green uniforms groveled alongside the Germans, echoing the cry for those debarking to make haste.

The disembarking passengers hardly noticed that huddling in a remote corner was a handful of Jewish police, easily mistaken for railway employees because they wore red conductor caps. Nor did the arriving Jews pay much attention to the four SS men in their black leather jackets smoking cigarettes who, with twisted grins planted on their frozen faces, regarded the people bustling and bumbling before them as one would chuckle at circus clowns tumbling over each other.

With the sun setting behind a distant line of trees, Sophie and Ludwig Frank detrained along with several hundred other German Jews. They and their fellow travelers were taken aback at the brusqueness with which they were treated. After all, Sophie thought, the transfer was to have been merely a change of address, or so she had been informed when she and her husband were ordered to pack their belongings and prepare to leave Germany. Sophie mulled this over as she replayed in her mind the scene from a few days earlier.

"Where are we going?" Sophie had asked, squaring her shoulders and stepping between the smug German officer and her husband who had retreated into the shadows of the lamp lighting their two-room residence in the Jewish quarter.

"To a lovely place called Theresienbad or, as some say, Theresienstadt am See," the young man said as if describing a lovely village on the lake. "It is like Carlsbad, Frau. Indeed, it is not far from Carlsbad. A health spa, Frau!" But Sophie detected a sinister glimmer in his black eyes, and the upturn of his thin lips was more a sneer than a smile. "Pack your suitcases with care," the blond soldier shouted over his shoulder as he departed.

Sophie had lived her entire life in Germany so she was anxious to learn all she could about where she and her husband were headed. After making a number of inquiries, she determined that Theresienstadt, a city located north of Prague and not far from the German border, had been recently designated a Jewish town for German-speaking Jews over sixty where they could live the remainder of their lives. In addition, Jews who had served the *Vaterland* in World War I and were disabled or decorated also qualified for residency. So being sent to dwell within my walls seemed logical, Sophie concluded, since Ludwig was a week away from his sixty-third birthday, a decorated War veteran, and still easily agitated due to the poison gas he had inhaled in the trenches. Moreover, the move seemed auspicious given the terrible rumors she had heard about the destinations in the East where most of her friends and family had been deported; becoming one of my residents appeared a much more desirable option.

At the train station, Sophie became apprehensive when everyone was instructed to line up for a medical inspection. She tugged at the short sleeve of her dress to try to cover her swollen arm where she injected herself daily with insulin for diabetes. Sophie worried that the disease might prevent her from being admitted into the town, but her fears were allayed when she saw the friendly face of the Jewish physician conducting the cursory examinations. She assumed the doctor was Jewish by the red and white armband he wore. In the center, *K. L. Terezín* was written while cursive letters running down the side spelled the name Dr. Reines. In a short time, Sophie and Ludwig would be assigned similar armbands with their names inscribed.

"Will I be able to secure insulin here?" Sophie asked after Dr. Reines noticed the bulge on her arm.

"I'm afraid not, Frau. But do not be concerned. The diet in *Terezín* works wonders on diabetics! None of the sweets and harmful foods that would raise your sugar are available." The physician forced a laugh, but seeing the bewilderment on Sophie's face, he returned to his task. She will learn soon enough what our diet is like, he thought. Dr. Reines appraised Ludwig with a glance and returned to Sophie. "You both can move on. No need for a ride on the truck. You two can walk with the rest."

With a wave of the physician's hand, Sophie and Ludwig were dismissed. Sophie, like so many of my other residents, was relieved to learn that this initial screening was not the feared selection process they had heard about in furtive whispers detailing how those deemed unfit were deported east. Sophie sighed with relief. The examination was only to see if she and Ludwig could walk to the town. Sophie took comfort thinking how considerate it was to provide transportation for those unable to make the hike.

After an hour, with typical German efficiency, the bulk of the newcomers were ordered into rows four abreast, and clutching their baggage, they commenced their trek to the new home I would provide, situated somewhere in the distant horizon. The procession bypassed the houses of the Czechoslovakian population and tramped directly in my direction.

As the wearied procession slowly skirted the swampland, Sophie shivered in the cold, damp air enveloping her. The deep moats surrounding my imposing granite ramparts intensified the dank smell and soggy atmosphere, causing the marchers to grumble as they plodded, still four abreast, under the archway leading inside.

Sophie didn't know what to expect. Would there be an official delegation to greet them? Would thousands of Jewish men and women be stirring about their business like any typical city? In my earlier days, I certainly had hoped to provide grand receptions, but I had given up on such pipe dreams for some time. I would have even been satisfied if Sophie could have seen the shadows of my inhabitants against lights flickering off the drawn sheets on the windows where they were having supper in their homes and perhaps preparing for bed. But this, too, was not to be. Like almost everything of importance, the matter was out of my control.

Every arrival day was the same with a strict curfew imposed by Commandant Seidel leaving Sophie, like the others passing through my walls for the first time, unprepared for what awaited. With night falling, Sophie and Ludwig gazed in a daze at the empty streets barren and void of human life as though they had entered a ghost town. The only sounds they heard were the shuffling of their own feet along the cobblestones and the occasional banging of luggage jarring against the pavement. Sophie had grown weary and her feet heavy so she was relieved when the procession came to a halt at the doorway of a bleak stone building that served as my absorption center.

As crestfallen as Sophie felt, had she arrived a few months earlier with the first transports of German Jews, I am afraid to say she would have been even more disappointed with her initial quarters. In those days, the search, or *schleusen* as it was called, was conducted in a makeshift area of casements with sloping passages leading upwards. Ultimately, the arrivals spilled into broad, long rooms where the search was undertaken. The temporary sleeping quarters were stables filled with hay where the people slept in rows. Sometimes, they would remain there for as long as a week until permanent facilities were assigned—as if anything about me could have ever be considered permanent!

But by fall when Sophie arrived, things had improved. Precise procedures were followed. One by one, names were matched to a list and crossed off as they entered the absorption center. Luggage was checked. All money and jewelry was confiscated including Ludwig's gold watch, which he had been given on his bar mitzvah a half-century earlier. Indeed, everything of any conceivable value was seized: medicine, scissors, blade sharpeners, flasks filled with cognac, cookies, and chocolate were commandeered. Physical examinations under the supervision of Dr. Reines were conducted, and once again, Sophie was assured she would fare well without her insulin injection.

With little to do but wait, Sophie studied her temporary quarters and committed them to memory so that when she closed her eyes in a vain attempt to sleep, she still could see the mold-covered walls and dim, craggy corners. She and Ludwig grew accustomed to the foul-smelling, clammy air and the stench of unwashed, unkempt bodies huddled so close together that shifts were assigned for sitting or lying on the sodden floors. Unlike Ludwig who had a full frame and stood over six feet, Sophie was slight of build and easily slipped into an open space. Fortunately, her dark hair was parted in the center and laid flat on her head, no longer fashionably piled high where it likely would have flown in the face of a nearby occupant. With a childlike confidence spreading across his full face, Ludwig settled in next to his wife.

Finally, at the end of the third day, the intake operation was complete. Although transports had only been arriving since June, by the end of that year, 109,000 Jews disembarked and entered my domain, making me their home. On New Year's Day 1943, more than half of these favored Jews were dead having succumbed to disease, beatings, execution, or transport east.

Before being discharged from the absorption center, there remained the matter of a proper orientation which was presented by one of the block elders. In Sophie's case, the information that would prove so crucial for her survival was provided by Fritz Janowitz. Fritz was one of my favorites to introduce me to each new group of arrivals because he took pride in anything even remotely Jewish. He had been an ardent supporter of Jewish nationalism from his days as a student and, ultimately, was put in charge of the Jewish youth organization in Reichenberg. In 1931, after his family's business closed, Fritz settled in Prague, but he moved seven years later to Zurich where he secured work. But his people silently beckoned when Czechoslovakia mobilized, and he returned to serve the Jewish community, placing himself in harm's way. It wasn't long before I became a home for Fritz, and he was conferred with the position of block elder in the Magdeburg barracks.

Fritz had this way about him that was open, warm, and sincere. Sophie saw it at once and was impressed with the young, handsome, and well-dressed man, thinking that maybe things weren't so bad after all. He spoke words of encouragement and went so far as to suggest a sense of humor wouldn't hurt. Above all, he implored my people to be patient; there was no rush; there was nowhere one had to go; things would come in time. He carefully explained how the institutions and authorities operated and fielded every question until no more hands were raised. As always, Fritz had done his job well.

Once the orientation was complete, everyone was given ration slips, an initial three-day allotment of moldy bread, new Roman numerals to replace the numbers previously assigned at embarkation to secure each identity, and directions to their respective living quarters. In the case of Sophie's group, the men were to be housed in the Sudeten barracks, an immense three-story building at my periphery, and the women and children were directed to the Hamburger and Dresden barracks, three-story buildings covering an entire block. Cries of protest and tears of anguish filled the absorption center as families were torn asunder. Such times were the most difficult for me to withstand—except, of course, for the transports east.

A wave of panic swept over Ludwig's face at the thought of being alone. Sophie saw the terror seize his azure eyes, and she insisted on speaking to someone in authority. She explained how her husband's hearing had been impaired by the incessant roar of canons when he had served his country. "He was decorated! Did you know that? And is this how he is to be repaid?" Sophie confronted the staff representative from the Council of Elders whose placid expression remained unchanged. There was nothing he could do even if he was so inclined, he informed her. But the German officer peering over his shoulder took interest.

"You say your husband was decorated, Frau?" Sophie looked up at the German officer, a man in his fifties with a gray mustache who, she thought, must have seen duty in the First World War.

"Yes," she answered. The German turned his sullen eyes toward Ludwig. Sophie detected a glint of recognition in his gaze that the Jew standing before him might have been one of his comrades with whom he had fought side by side in the trenches. The German whispered into the Jewish official's ear. The Jewish bureaucrat shrugged and wrote new instructions on a slip of paper.

Before leaving the absorption center, all luggage was returned though considerably lighter after being pilfered by the Germans and Czechs. Sophie grimaced at this turn of events, but actually, she was quite fortunate. While there were a few transports where my arrivals received their suitcases intact, in many cases, all personal belongings vanished into thin air, never to be seen again. It really was a matter of providence whether anything was returned at all. Finally, like everyone else, Sophie and Ludwig were given their bedrolls and sent on their way.

After wandering the ghetto's dark streets for more than an hour, Sophie and Ludwig located their living quarters in a building crammed with families consisting of the staff serving the Council of Elders. Climbing three flights of narrow, creaking stairs, a seemingly endless area presented itself, though it was difficult to gauge the size of the room because sections were cordoned off by hanging sheets separating one family from the next.

People were scurrying everywhere, but no one took the time to greet them or even acknowledge their presence. A cacophony of languages caused Sophie's head to swirl. Many spoke High German, but as Sophie and Ludwig sidled through the throng, Sophie could tell from dialects that many of the Jews were from Bohemia and Moravia. Later, the dormitory would also be home to Jews from the Netherlands, Hungary, Luxembourg, and Denmark.

Just as Sophie was about to give up securing a place to sleep, she spotted an unoccupied space in a far corner that was perhaps two meters by two meters. A ragged mattress was precariously balanced on a makeshift box spring and pushed against the moldy wall. There was barely enough room for Ludwig and Sophie to stand after they plopped their luggage on the musty floor. But they would make do, Sophie resolved, staring wide-eyed at what would be their home for the next two and a half years.

Except for the one time the Red Cross visited the ghetto, daily life remained virtually unchanged. Though I had little to offer in the way of comfort and conveniences, I did provide a sense of security to my people in the knowledge they could expect things to proceed with predictability day to day, week to week, and even year to year if they lived that long. So every morning, Sophie and Ludwig knew to queue up for a breakfast of ersatz coffee and their daily allotment of a half loaf of black bread. In the afternoon, they were served either a tasteless lentil soup made from dried ground or a weak soup called *wrucken* consisting of white turnips and a mixture of sand, dirt, and a trace of flour to give it substance. Sipping her cup of ersatz coffee, Sophie took consolation that the absence of sugar would indeed keep her diabetes in check.

Eventually, Sophie and Ludwig grew accustomed to the cold, damp air and the incessant gnawing of an empty stomach. But the loss of privacy was another matter. Sophie and Ludwig had always valued their time alone, and losing it was perhaps the most difficult adjustment to make. People were everywhere, perpetually scrambling about and falling over one another. The courtyards were constantly crowded with long lines of sunken faces and haunting eyes waiting to be fed, receive rations, or petition the Council for some special request. To Sophie's amazement, there was also the clamor and shouting of children at play. Sophie delighted in watching the small youngsters prance and run about, and she prayed they would remain oblivious to their fate.

Sophie and Ludwig fell into a routine, keeping busy from morning until night. Sophie was assigned to tend the gardens, which the Council of Elders hoped would provide fresh vegetables for the populace. Sophie had always loved her gardens at home, and with that experience she proved herself helpful in making my gardens flourish, something which brought me much pride. Ludwig, on the other hand, like many of the men, did not have the practical experience that I sorely needed in order to function. He had been a cattle broker, and with no cattle, let alone a market for them, he was of little use to me and had to be assigned to maintenance details. Naturally, he was not happy performing menial work, but eventually, he accepted his new lot in life. Ludwig took matters day by day and had little interests in the goings-on of the ghetto other than what directly effected his immediate needs.

Sometimes, late in the afternoon or in the early evening hours, a singer or musician filled the air with song and music. Entertainment and cultural activities became periodic events with a symphony performing on a regular basis. Several studios were established, and a makeshift library boasted so many volumes that most municipalities would have been jealous. Some of my most rewarding accomplishments were the cultural and educational programs I afforded, and I'll speak more of this later.

But of all the activities established within my walls, most precious to Sophie was the vibrant religious life I provided, and despite all she had endured and was yet to bear, she never lost her faith in God. This was something that always amazed me, and Sophie was not alone in holding steadfast to her religious beliefs. I cannot say the same for myself. Having been conceived at a time when the destruction of an entire race was ordained, I never experienced anything that would give me even the slightest hint that there existed a benevolent providence to which prayers might be directed and comfort and justice sought. Yet, I could understand the believers in my midst since they were a part of me, and I was able to visualize how, before she reached my walls, Sophie would set a *Shabbas* dinner every Friday evening with a special white tablecloth, candles, challah, wine, and snuffbox. Her home was open to any stranger or visitor traveling through the tiny town of Odenbach where she lived. On the high holidays, she wore her finest dress when she accompanied Ludwig, himself accoutered in tails and a top hat, to travel to the synagogue in Frankfurt.

Before 1933, most German Jews, while never reticent about their Jewish faith, adhered to the maxim: Jewish in the home. German in the street. Sophie and Ludwig belonged to a Conservative synagogue rather than a Reform-oriented temple, but they harbored no ill will towards those joining the more modern branch of Judaism.

So who was I to stand in their way? In Theresienstadt, daily services of all sorts were conducted in clandestine locations out of the watchful eye of the Czech and Nazi guards. Sophie and Ludwig would attend whenever they had the opportunity, and she particularly enjoyed the sermons and lectures. Services were led by rabbis, cantors, or laymen. But the formality of an organized prayer service that Sophie found comforting was largely absent; the lack of a leader left a void in the community. A Moses was needed to provide spiritual life if this remnant of Jewry was to survive intact. Sophie sensed this need, and less than three months after her arrival, her hopes for such a man were realized.

On January 27, 1943, the last Jews from Berlin marched under my archway. As they tramped through the streets, word quickly spread that Rabbi Baeck had arrived. Despite the usual curfew, people ventured out to see the man who had been the former chief rabbi of Berlin and spiritual leader of Germany's Jews, a man who refused opportunities to flee Germany, choosing instead to remain, a man who resolutely declared that he would emigrate only when he was "the last Jew alive in Germany."

Sophie was more circumspect, and she secured a spot by a window, not risking a curfew violation. But she had no trouble discerning Dr. Leo Baeck at the forefront of the slowly moving throng. In fact, with his high forehead and white hair, Baeck reminded Sophie of Moses leading the Hebrews out of slavery and into years of wandering before reaching freedom and the Promised Land. How ironic, I thought at the time, that this Moses is leading his people into slavery, and how many more years will it be until any of them regain their freedom, if ever.

But the circumstances did not diminish the majesty of the man. Though almost seventy, each step Baeck took was made with determination and purpose, the same gait and demeanor he would display when pushing the garbage cart or a hearse stacked with potatoes and bread through my streets, always taking time to stop and consider a question put before him by some passerby. And when he answered, he spoke with the identical tone and thoughtfulness he employed when delivering a sermon to his congregation or a lecture to a group of rabbis and scholars. Articulated in a high-pitched voice, each word was chosen with care, building sentences that flowed with equal rhythm in a steady, unbroken current. To emphasize a point, Baeck would gesture with his hand or narrow his eyes as if an arrow was about to be shot from a bow.

I came to learn more of the man beneath the public persona, the mere mortal removed from the pedestal upon which his people had placed him. The austere and confidant exterior belied his inner suffering, torment, and doubts. Like most Germans, Baeck kept his troubles to himself. Such things were private matters, not meant to be turned into a public display. For instance, he had hoped to be reunited with his four sisters whom I had received months earlier, but to his dismay, when he arrived only one was still alive, and she died soon thereafter. Nor had his heart fully recovered following the death of his wife shortly before he began his journey to reach me. And how he still missed the trips to London where he visited with his daughter when escorting groups of children for relocation in England. On such excursions, his daughter pleaded with him to remain with her. There was no longer any future for the Jews in Germany, she argued. His life was already in danger; she need not have reminded him. What was there to return to? To which Baeck always made the same resolute reply, "As long as there is a *minyan* to be served, I will return." But no one would have known any of this from his outward appearance.

Despite Baeck's humility, he was not unmindful of his position of leadership. As the former president of the *Reichsvertretung*, the representative body of German Jews, Baeck was immediately acknowledged by the Council of Elders and declared its honorary president. Naturally, the Council could not allow so distinguished a man to reside in the common barracks swarming with people like bees in a beehive, so Baeck was assigned a small, albeit dreary, room in one of the houses of the prominents.

While I never approved of this practice that resulted in some of my people receiving special privileges such as private living quarters and extra food rations, I understand that it is human nature to create class distinctions. But given that in the end, the Germans looked upon all my occupants, prominents included, as being nothing more than subhuman creatures no better than vermin, and almost all would suffer the same fate, I would have preferred no self-created divisions among my people and had hoped they would consider themselves as being simply Jews—one and all.

Like all the prominents, Baeck accepted his favored treatment without giving it much thought. He simply went about transforming his living quarters into a sanctum where he could continue to work on his book, *This People*. Writing books was important to Baeck and for good reason because it was a book he authored in 1905, *The Essence of Judaism,* that placed him at the forefront of German Jewry. Baeck wrote that book in response to Adolf von Harnack's *The Essence of Christianity* which had compared Judaism unfavorably to Christianity. While a vocal advocate for mutual tolerance among the world's religions, in *The Essence of Judaism,* Baeck took up the defense of Judaism, emphasizing its ethical action in contrast to what he believed was the emotion and grace of Christianity.

There were other factors, however, that made Baeck a popular figure among my residents. For one, there was his diverse background. The son of a rabbi raised in a traditional home, Baeck had attended a Conservative rabbinical academy, but he subsequently transferred to Berlin's Reform-oriented Higher Institute for Jewish Studies where the religious curriculum was complemented by philosophical studies. In 1897, he received his rabbinic diploma, and he served at congregations in Silesia and Dusseldorf before becoming rabbi of the Oranienburger Street Synagogue in Berlin.

Though lacking a convivial and dynamic personality, Baeck's integrity and scholarship, as well as his previous positions of leadership, made him a much sought after figure during his stay. On a regular basis, people would gather in the barracks to hear him lecture on Plato, Kant, Aristotle, Spinoza, and Herodotus.

Accustomed to the burdens of responsibility and leadership, Baeck assumed the yoke of his new position with acceptance, though nothing in his roles as rabbi, educator, spiritual leader, or simply one more inmate pushing a cart through my streets prepared him for the profound moral dilemma he was confronted with that August.

It began well before Baeck's arrival in January of 1943. Rumors of all sorts were abounding, furtively whispered in the alleys or spoken in hushed tones in the barracks. Voices at once both incredulous and fearful posited the possibility that those boarding the transports leaving the Bauschowitz station for Lithuania and Latvia were shot to death upon their arrival. Speculations were made that in Auschwitz, where many transports were destined, those not found fit for labor or some other useful purpose were killed by gas. At times, some suggested, the trains simply stopped in a remote spot, and the people were driven out to be shot or herded into enclosed vans and gassed.

But this was mere gossip, was it not? Based on wild imagination and fear. Or so I thought…at first. Most believed the Germans were a civilized people despite their anti-Semitism. They would not carry out such atrocities. Nonetheless, at the prodding of the Council of Elders seeking some reassurances, Edelstein diffidently raised the question with Seidl for corroboration. Stroking back his wavy, dark hair and sliding his glasses over the bridge of his nose, Edelstein asked the commandant if, as some had heard, Jews on the transports were gassed. Without hesitation, Seidl declared, "I have no idea of such a thing!"

Edelstein darted back to the Council's offices, anxious to assure the members that there was no basis to the rumors. Seidl had always been forthright, had he not? Edelstein asked, seeking out the anxious faces around the table for confirmation. The transports go to labor camps, he continued. And while conditions may be harsh, and people die from work, malnutrition, and disease, as some do even here, he pointed out, they are not murdered. There still remains life and hope, he concluded.

Nonetheless, the rumors persisted, and the shootings and gassings lingered in the back of everyone's mind. If only the issue could be put to rest one way or the other; if only someone whom everyone believed and trusted proclaimed whether or not it was so. Such a moment presented itself in August 1943 with a knock on the door of Rabbi Baeck's room. Opening the door, Baeck encountered the face of a stranger. The man hesitated for a moment and then introduced himself as a Czech engineer by the name of Grunberg. Baeck bid the man to enter. Grunberg appeared anxious and asked in a muted voice if they could speak in confidence. Baeck assured him he could.

The men sat down in the cramped quarters, and as Grunberg related what he had learned, the rabbi's shoulders sagged lower and lower with each new piece of information foisted upon him. One night, Grunberg began, he had been shaken from his sleep by the appearance of a good friend whom he had not seen for years. Because his friend was half Jewish, he had been sent to Auschwitz where he was put to labor. While there, he found out about the gas chambers. Fearful that at the end of the day he would also be gassed, he made an escape and returned to Prague where he bribed a Czech policeman to allow him to enter Theresienstadt so he could warn Grunberg of the fate that awaited him and the other Jews.

"But who will believe me?" Grunberg asked, looking imploringly at Baeck. Hence, he explained, he had decided to seek out the revered rabbi whom almost everyone would certainly heed.

Baeck accepted what Grunberg said. There had been too many reports of the gas chambers in Auschwitz to deny an eyewitness account from someone who risked his life to convey the message. But what to do? Baeck rested his head against his hand, stroking his white mustache and goatee with his forefinger. His eyebrows arched over the clear frames of his spectacles while he pondered the quandary put before him.

He knew that once he informed the Council of Elders, it would be only a matter of hours before word of the gas chambers would spread like wildfire and engulf the camp. And what good would come of it? As Baeck would recount in his memoirs, "Living in the expectation of death by gassing would be all the harder. And this death was not certain for all." Best to live in the hope that freedom and life lay ahead, which for some might even come to pass, he concluded.

Baeck told no one of the confirmation of Auschwitz's gas chambers. It was a decision that weighed heavily upon him every day but one which he resolutely held. In later years, some criticized him, but most of my survivors were grateful and supported his action.

Despite Baeck's predisposition towards candor, recent circumstances had taught him that it is sometimes best to keep certain suspicions to himself in order to spare his people further pain. As the president of the *Reichsvertretung*, Baeck had been wary of the deceptive ploy the Third Reich utilized to convince the German Jews destined for Theresienstadt that it was a spa-like resort where they would peacefully spend the rest of their days. The Third Reich's audacity knew no bounds in creating this subterfuge, a precursor of their ultimate achievement when presenting me to the Red Cross as a showcase town, demonstrating to the entire world how kind Germany was to its Jews.

In crafting this deceit to lure German Jewry to my granite ramparts, contracts were carefully drafted and executed with each future resident of Theresienbad providing that all their liquid assets would be conveyed to the Jewish Federation. In exchange, each resident was guaranteed a lifelong residence that included food, laundry, medical treatment, and drugs. Of course, the money was never transferred to the Jewish Federation but instead diverted to the Reich Security Head Office as had been planned all along. Naturally, eyebrows were raised by the officials of the Federation when they never received the funds, but given the circumstances, there was nothing they could do.

These old German Jews were so convinced that the Third Reich's representations were genuine that they packed their finest apparel, mementos, and jewelry when they should have taken eating utensils and blankets instead. With each arrival of German Jews at the Bauschowitz station, the same scene played out again and again: eager conversations about seeing old friends; people speculating about the possibility of obtaining a suite facing the lake; high expectations expressed over the wonderful food and taking in the comforts of the spa's waters.

But gradually, the enthusiasm subsided with each batch of newcomers slowly making the approach to my looming ramparts. The happy chatter at the train station was replaced by silence and then by grumbles and finally complaints as the truth unfolded. There were even official protests made that the contract, which some of the new arrivals still clutched in their hands, had been breached and that legal action must be taken. Imagine that! These people actually thought they could sue the German government, the very same government that, a decade earlier, had stripped them of their rights as citizens. I confess having had difficulty indulging them this delusion, and I still can't decide whether it emanated from hubris or an innate belief their former country would one day come to its senses and accept them back.

Indeed, no one was more shocked than Jakob Edelstein at the subterfuge. He gasped in amazement when several of the contracts were waved in his face by furious supplicants. But what did they expect him to do? He shrugged. Do something! The red-faced newcomers demanded. A ghetto with barracks is not what we paid for! With a deep sigh, Edelstein gathered several of the formal-looking documents together, shoved them in his jacket pocket, and darted down his regular route to Seidl's quarters for his daily meeting.

Edelstein thought he detected a smirk on Seidl's face as the commandant perused one of the contracts, holding it up to the light. "Well?" Edelstein asked. Setting the paper down on his desk and straightening his shoulders, Seidl gave his official pronouncement with the same aloofness and disinterest he employed at any question or request put to him by the Elder of the Jews, as Edelstein had come to be called.

"I'll report the matter to Berlin," said Seidl. And with that, as far as the German authorities were concerned, the matter was closed.

But for Edelstein and the Council of Elders, the matter was far from closed. How were they expected to make Theresienstadt habitable for the tens of thousands of German Jews, almost all of whom were over sixty, unable to work, and who presented the Council with more mouths to feed, bodies to clothe, and souls to tend to.

The sheer numbers were daunting. In the months following the night Sophie and Ludwig tramped under my archway, the population swelled to 30,000, then 40,000, and finally 50,000 inmates. The density was so severe that there was less than five square feet of living space per resident. Old men dressed in black suits were assigned to keep watch over the toilets and outhouses to ensure no one took too long since there was only one toilet for every 100 persons. The wood supply ran out, and bunks could not be built. Food provisions were wholly inadequate and the boiler capacity insufficient to prepare meals. Disease and death became a way of life.

As I have said, these aged German and Austrian Jews of the Reich arrived woefully unprepared. What items they still retained that had not been confiscated were generally inappropriate to the conditions of ghetto life. To make matters even worse, if that was possible, most of the elderly had no one to look after them since many had sent their children to safety in foreign lands. They were too old for work, and yet, they could be demanding. While I understood how Edelstein and his colleagues sometimes bristled at the arrogance of these new arrivals, their occasional intolerance still troubled me. But soon enough, their hardened hearts softened at the sight of these wretched souls moping about dazed, confused, and disillusioned with the situation into which they were cast. In the end, they came to realize they were all in it together, and Jew looked after Jew because there was no one else who would.

Once the recent arrivals settled in, things fell into place. Still attired in the once-fine-but-now-frayed apparel in which they had arrived, these old Jews could be seen queued in line, grasping tin containers in their wrinkled hands, patiently waiting for their small ration of ersatz coffee and lentil soup or *wrucken*. And if a younger person in front, who was given a larger allotment of bread and other vitals because of a more demanding work assignment, declined the ladle with the watery broth, one of these older men or women might tap him on the shoulder and humbly ask if he could spare his portion of soup.

How could one feel anything but compassion at the sight of these aged Jews wandering the streets, some of whom could not even remember the return route to their barracks? Or empathize with the helpless, hunched bodies meandering about, stricken by night-blindness because they lacked the necessary vitamins in their diet? Or stooped and twisted figures slogging along the cobblestone streets with nothing else to do but try to ignore the unaccustomed pangs of hunger they endured while waiting for their next meal?

Indeed, as my demographics shifted with the steady stream of elderly Jews, I discovered that I underwent a metamorphosis of my own. I detected listlessness in the goings-on about me, an unaccustomed weariness to my spirit; strength had to be summoned merely to face the rising sun and dawn of each new day. My role as a self-sustaining city for the Jews of the Protectorate where hardly anyone was over forty-five and almost everyone was able to work had been re-configured to that of an old-age home where the majority of my residents were above sixty and very few could perform even the most minimal task or light labor.

Nor did it help matters that to make room for the arrival of the elderly German Jews, the younger Czech Jews had to be selected for transport east. This was the new German directive, and there was no way the Council of Elders could avoid its implementation. Even the friends and relatives of Council members were at risk of being placed on the notorious list in order to make room for strangers who did not even speak their language.

If this was not enough, the final stake driven into the hearts and minds of the Czech Jews to create splinters and divisions among my people was the order from Eichmann himself that six of the twelve members on the Council of Elders were to be replaced by Jews from the Reich (two from Vienna and four from Berlin). Edelstein found himself with a new deputy, Heinrich Stahl, the former chairman of Berlin's

Jewish community. It was hard not to resent these new arrivals whom the Germans clearly considered to be superior to the Czech Jews.

A hierarchy of sorts was thus established by the Germans, which caused me great anguish, and yet, I was helpless to do anything about it. Placed at the top by the Germans were the German Jews because as parasitic as all Jews were, at least these Jews had benefited from the centuries they dwelled on German soil, experiencing German culture. The German Jews were followed by the Austrian Jews, and then came the Czech Jews. In the years to follow, Jews from other nations would plod into the camp, and other than those from Denmark, all would be considered even more inferior.

But the thread that had been woven through the mosaic of the Jewish people during their 2,000-year Diaspora when they were forced to live as strangers in foreign lands remained resilient. The Jews of Moravia and Bohemia bonded with the Jews of Germany and Austria and later with the Jews from Denmark, Hungary, the Netherlands, and near the end, the survivors from camps in the East—so that as one people, they tried their best to survive the living hell that came to be called the Paradise Ghetto.

CHAPTER SEVEN: THE CHILDREN

Most of the children who would come to think of me as home approached me in the same manner as the adults—by way of the Bauschowitz train station followed by the seemingly endless trek to my granite fortress façade. Of course, there were differences. Invariably, every small child held tightly to the grip of a grown-up, allowing his or her hand to be firmly grasped and occasionally squeezed with assurance that all is well. If need be, for additional support, the boy or girl might glance up, seeking solace from the face of a parent, older sibling, or some other adult who, after all, must know what is going on, and in reply, there would be a downward look and perhaps a smile or even words of encouragement: "Just a little further…not so bad a walk, eh? Hungry? You'll be fed soon, just wait and see. Tired? In a little while, we'll rest and sleep." And if, for some reason, nothing had been forthcoming, another tug at the hand would almost always ensure a reassuring response.

I cannot imagine how frightening I must have appeared to the children when I first came into sight; a mysterious citadel in the distance unlike anything they had ever seen before: massive, towering, a fetid smell emanating from the moat surrounding me. And as I drew closer in the dark and heavy mist, I must have presented myself as a sinister specter, stoking their worst fears and unbridled imaginations into horrible things to come.

For some of these children, however, there was no need for imagination. An all too vivid reality had spawned memories that would not go away no matter how hard they tried. Such was the case in August 1943 when a transport arrived packed with children from the Bialystok ghetto, which had recently been destroyed. Some of these children had seen their parents shot before their eyes; others were wrenched from the arms of their mothers and fathers who were being taken to "showers" from which they never returned. The last sight many held of their parents was a forlorn gaze transmitting despair, fear, resignation, love, affection, and a promise that things will be all right.

When these children were escorted to my shower room, their eyes expanded in dread accompanied by terrifying screams of panic ricocheting like bullets clamoring off of the tiled walls. The boys and girls struggled to free themselves from the adults, nurses, and doctors hovering over them and trying to calm them but to no avail. Finally, the children made themselves understood in Yiddish that the showers meant death, confirmation that the rumors were indeed true; Jews were being gassed by the Nazis.

Every effort was made to assuage these young ones and bring them some sense of security. They were taken to a new barracks in Kreta, a suburb just outside my ramparts, accompanied by two doctors and fifty-two nurses and instructors. Special food was provided, and after six weeks, most had gained significant weight. The fear on their faces faded; occasionally, there were even smiles. They were given fresh clothes without the yellow star, and they were informed by the German Authority that they could leave for the free world accompanied by their nurses and teachers.

"All you need to do, *meine kinder,*" the smiling German officer said, "is sign the form that you will not discuss anything you witnessed in Bialystok." And the children believed this. Eager, youthful hands signed the documents given to them by the German soldiers. All would be well, they were assured. A train to freedom will follow and then later, a ship and voyage at sea to America or Palestine or England. But that, of course, was a ruse; the transport did not head west but rather east to Birkenau where each and every boy and girl was gassed.

On the other hand, there were some youngsters who took me in stride because they knew no home other than the one I provided. These were the children born within my walls, the first of whom arrived in mid-February 1942, a boy by the name of Thomas who became known as A-K One. He was called A-K because the first influx of Jews from Prague to reach me and prepare me for occupancy were known as A-K units, and Thomas, being the first born in my realm, appropriately enough bore the additional designation of One. This is not to say that this practice continued for long, as I do not recall an A-K Nine or an A-K thirty.

Children under the age of four generally lived with their mothers. Subsequently, they were assigned to dwell in a children's home, really a barracks, where they lived in the lifestyle of a collective, reflecting the socialist leanings of my early denizens. Not only did these dormitories separate boys from girls, but once German Jews began to arrive, the Czech children resided in barracks apart from the German children. In part, this was because of language difficulties, but in time, the barriers among the various nationalities broke down as the children participated in sports, attended concerts, and played soccer together.

With the past irretrievably lost and the present unbearably onerous, all that remained for my people was the future, and while ominous for themselves, they gathered all their hopes and dreams and placed them upon the children. Thus, every effort was extended to make the lives of the youngsters more endurable in my milieu and prepare them to rejoin the world of the living after the War.

In terms of daily activities, the children were permitted to play in the gardens and courtyards, areas generally off-limits to adults, thus affording an opportunity where they could amuse themselves on my fortifications and fantasize a better and more vibrant life. The kitchen staff extended their efforts to serve the children more palatable food. The children even had their own hospital operated by the Youth Welfare Department.

But as I said, the chief concern was that the children be able to succeed when they reenter society. Of course, I sometimes questioned whether this was even remotely a realistic expectation. But there was little left for my people to look forward to, and how could I deny them this prospect; after all, weren't optimism and hope essential ingredients of human nature without which one would not be able to make it from one day to the next? Hence, emphasis was placed upon education, and while formal classes were banned by the German authorities, an admirable quality of instruction was achieved with schooling provided up to the age of fifteen.

At first, the Czechs were determined to construct a curriculum based upon a Czech national education, but they reluctantly conceded this was not practical once Jews from other countries began to comprise my populace. As a result, lessons were conducted in Czech, German, and Hebrew. Teaching was both formal and informal, carried out in the adult lecture halls, the children's dormitories, in hallways and attics, sometimes even out of doors with sentries on the look-out. Since all adults had their respective work assignments, and officially, education could not be one of them, most classes were held in the evenings and on Saturday mornings. But despite the obstacles, learning thrived in my world.

The curriculum was impressive with a basic education in the humanities, social science, and the arts. Science presented a unique challenge since it was difficult to teach without the benefit of a laboratory. There was a children's newspaper, *We Lead*; its editor, Peter Ganz, first walked under my archway at the age of fourteen, alone and without his parents.

Once the elderly began filling my population, the counselors organized a project called "Helping Hand," whereby the children visited the old people's rooms three times per week. It was so moving to observe the old and the young reach out to one another; one hand, pale and withered, trembling as its purplish veins press against paper-thin skin, grasping the spotless, smaller hand, its fingers fluttering like the wings of a butterfly. Once contact was achieved, though tenuous at first, a firm grip would take hold, and for a moment, the two appendages melded into one. This scene repeated itself over and over, and never did I grow weary of it.

It was not only the elderly who benefited from the children. Frequently, the youth organization performed dance recitals and gymnastics for the entire adult population in the parade ground known as the bastion. The bastion was laid out as a quadrangle with ramparts on three sides and the Jager barracks serving as the fourth. A mighty tree dominated the square and served as a canopy for the stage upon which the children performed.

Like a breath of fresh air or a sunny spring day, the children lit up the lives of those in attendance. Wearing white shirts and dark trousers, they performed with precision. With their crimson cheeks and sparkling eyes and the zest with which they sprang about the stage, the audience voraciously devoured the fleeting illusion of normalcy, and for this I was forever grateful to the young artistes.

Never to miss an opportunity, the Nazis took advantage of the talent the children had developed, and it was decided to exploit my youngest inmates to help convince the world just how wonderful a milieu I provided. By order from Commandant Rahm, the opera *Brundibár*, also known as *The Organ Grinder*, was to be performed by the children in the Magdeburg barracks with the setting adapted from the performance that had been staged in the Prague Orphanage. The premiere was held on September 23, 1943 with Rahm himself in attendance, beaming at the youthful players whom, he said, were clearly "thriving" under his tutelage. The children posed for a photo to publicize the event; fifty youngsters, dressed in their costumes, stood stiffly with their arms at their sides. The Germans were so pleased that not only was the photograph brazenly displayed for the world to see, but they included film of the production in their propaganda movie made the following year.

But if one were to look closely, the truth could not be hidden. Most of the children appeared somber, and those few who made the effort to pose as instructed did so with forced, frozen smiles. Many of the children looked away from the camera; one boy, who stood out in the back row because he was tall, had closed his eyes, pouted his lips, and made a disgruntled face. Finally, no matter what angle or distance the photographer chose, one glaring fact stood out from the photograph that the Germans could not conceal; despite efforts to provide additional nourishment to the children, the emaciated torsos of the youngsters bore testament to the truth.

The younger children lived a sheltered life, at least to the extent possible under the circumstances. They were fed better food and had more privileges than all other inmates, but upon reaching the age of fourteen, they were treated as adults and were apprenticed for work. In the summer months when everyone shed their heavy winter clothing, the adolescent girls could be seen in the early dawn hours wearing colorful skirts of light material and bright blouses, multihued kerchiefs on their heads or tied around their necks, marching four or five astride to report for roll call to pick up their buckets and brooms for the day's work.

Eleven children's homes were established where the youngsters were housed by year of birth in different rooms. Male and female guardians known as room leaders were assigned to each room to mentor and teach the children. For example, there was L 410 for Czech girls ages eight to sixteen while L 414 was home to both German and Czech girls ages ten to fourteen. Unfortunately, the Czech girls became estranged from the German girls because the latter spoke the language of the oppressors. Once again, to my dismay, there was division among my people, and soon the children were housed according to nationality and language.

Outside L 410, where Czech girls resided and which had once been the camp headquarters in the market square, Friedl Dicker-Brandeis lived in a little shed in the courtyard. Friedl's shed, as it became known, was inconspicuous enough from the exterior, but inside, it was another story and a reflection of its occupant. A dyed-blue cloth on which pictures were stitched covered the walls. Sometimes a vase with flowers stood on a table—an oasis in a barren land, much like Friedl herself who played a similar role for her girls.

Friedl was forty-four when she reached my ramparts in December 1942 along with her husband, Pavel. She was a woman with shortly cropped, thick, black hair above a prominent forehead. Full lips and a thickset nose seemed out of place on her narrow face, but it was her eyes that attracted attention; large and round, they were deeply set below heavy eyelids and resided just above her omnipresent darkened bags which evinced a constant weariness and chronic fatigue.

Friedl had been born into a middle-class Viennese family and was destined to be the only child after her mother died when Friedl was three. Raised by her father, she was trained as an artist, and by the time she was deported, she was recognized as a most talented and progressive one at that. In my realm, she organized classes for the children and encouraged them to seek an escape from reality by looking out the window, a phrase she was fond of saying. "Look out the window, child…just look out the window." Alas, less than two years after arriving, looking out the window failed Friedl, and she was unable to avoid the ultimate escape; she and Pavel were placed on a transport to Auschwitz where they were killed soon after their arrival.

But while she was with me, Friedl touched countless lives and in particular, the girls of Room 28, who became known as Friedl's Girls. The occupants of Room 28, situated in Children's House L 410, hailed from Bohemia and Moravia and came from upper- and middle-class backgrounds. What all the girls had in common was that they were students of Friedl.

Of course, Friedl favored some of the girls more than others; she was only human. While all the girls were her students, only a few would have the opportunity to study with her privately. The audition was informal, and the determination in the case of Marta Frohlich was fairly typical of how Friedl made her selections.

Marta was a girl with very short, brown hair, a prominent forehead, and a long, thin neck. What drew people to her was her vivacious smile, but Friedl was not interested in that.

"Draw some lines," Friedl commanded. Marta complied. "Now, what do you suppose you could make out of those lines?"

"I…I don't know," Marta stammered.

"But surely you see something there!" Friedl pronounced with a nod to the lines on the paper. Marta became confused, her forehead crinkled while her small eyes squinted at the sheet. Friedl bent over the page and rotated it one way, then another, each time asking Marta, "Do you see anything yet?" Marta shook her head in growing frustration. Finally, Friedl suggested that Marta think about one of the picture books she had examined earlier. Thoughtfully, Marta pursed her lips, and then a shock of recognition spread across her face as the vision of a dancing woman passed over her mind's eye, and she drew a dancer based on the lines. "Yes!" Friedl smiled. "You have talent, and you can now study with me."

The unofficial symbol of Room 28 was a flag with the image of the *Maagal,* two hands in a tight grip that had been inspired by Tella Pollak, the room leader. The *Maagal* flag lasted for quite some time until a group of the girls was ordered to be deported to the East. Meeting together for the last time in their dormitory, which had come to be a haven from an unsafe world, they tore the flag into quarters. Huddling together in a circle, the girls passed the frayed sections among themselves, vowing aloud that after the war they would reunite and stitch it back together. Furtive glances and knowing stares made their way from one girl to the next. Ultimately, the frail but resolute young women nodded in silence. Sharing the same fate as the girls, only one piece survived the war.

Tella Pollak, the person most responsible for creating the *Maagal,* was an effervescent young woman whose features manifested her personality. Her prominent cheekbones stood out from under a canopy of lustrous, brunette hair and bushy eyebrows. Her thin lips created a triangular smile that sailed over a square jaw jutting out in both defiance and determination to win the day. Like the banner she helped craft, she herself served as a beacon of hope to many of her roommates, especially Anna Flach and Lenka Lindt.

As was common with many of the girls, Anna was affectionately addressed by her nickname, Flaska. Her curly, light brown hair that parted on the left was often adorned with a white bow, a trademark of hers. She was a petite girl with narrow eyes and an infectious grin who loved to draw pencil-on-paper sketches. Unlike most of her roommates, Flaska survived the war.

One day in October 1944, a new list was posted with names of those selected for transport east. Anxiously, Flaska craned her neck through the cracks in the shoulders and heads of those in front of her. She was relieved to see her name was not listed, but her heart dropped when she spotted Lenka's name on the list. Elbowing her way out of the crowd, she darted down the cobbled streets in search for her friend.

Finding her, she asked Lenka to please write an entry in her memory book. Lenka inscribed in part, "One is born into this world to do good. Whoever does otherwise has no right to be a human being. Do what Tella taught us...Remember this, my dear friend."

Lenka was murdered shortly after reaching Auschwitz, dead at the age of fourteen. Transformed into ashes, her body's remains vanished into the black sky, chimneys spewing the residue of the corpses into their celestial graves. But Lenka's poems did not succumb; they lived on. Many years later, one of her roommates, Eva Landau, who had been twelve when assigned to Room 28, came upon two of Lenka's poems contained in a notebook which she had purchased in Prague many years after the war. How astounded she was to find they had been dedicated to her!

Eva had also been inspired by Tella to do good deeds, and it was not long before the twelve-year-old took it upon herself to assist my more recent elderly arrivals—even if it meant nothing more than bringing them a glass of water. Sometimes, these new residents raised wary eyes or backed away, suspicious of the smiling, pug-nosed girl with blond, wavy hair making her appear to be the perfect Aryan. But once they realized she was one of them, her help and kindness was gratefully accepted.

There is a favorite in every group, and as for the girls of Room 28, no one was more popular than Ruth Schachter. Ruth's nickname, Zajieek, meant "bunny," likely because of her large, protruding teeth, which she tried to conceal by closing her mouth, especially when smiling. Zajieek was adored by everyone and grateful for any kind word, but her sojourn with me was not an easy one. Her parents fled to Palestine where they hoped to settle and then send for their two children at the earliest opportunity. The plan was that in the interim, Zajieek and her brother would remain in an orphanage in Brno, but before their parents could make the arrangements to retrieve them to safety, they were snatched away and sent to me. Zajieek remained one of my children until May 1944 when she was transported to Auschwitz where she died five months later.

Like the poems written by Lenka and the sketches drawn by Marta, many of the girls of Room 28 were artists in one way or another. Ela Stein, a brunette-haired girl with thick, dark eyebrows and a broad nose, was perfect for the role she played as the cat in fifty-five performances of the children's opera *Brundibár*. Helga Pollak, a slight girl with a long, thin neck reminding me of a swan, crafted pencil-on-paper pictures. Helga was sent to Auschwitz in October 1944 along with another girl from Room 28, Hanka Wertheimer.

Many of these young people were placed on transports east, clinging to the hope that they would somehow stay alive. In fact, a group of the girls from Room 28 took an oath to meet after the war in Prague's old town square at noon just in front of the clock tower. Some of the girls of Room 28, like Helga and Hanka, survived the mass murders; most did not.

Those charged with the task of caring for and educating the children made herculean efforts to create an atmosphere where the boys and girls could lead a normal life and be spared not only the physical suffering but also the emotional and psychological trauma engendered by their circumstances; nonetheless, the children could not be fooled. Sometimes, I suspect these young people, wise beyond their years, knew much more than they let on and played along with the charade, not wanting to disappoint the adults. But clues did exist, signifying that they had a rather good idea about the reality of where they lived and what might lie ahead in their future, even though sometimes these signs were quite subtle.

Take for example the monopoly game the children themselves created and played. The properties were named after landmarks and buildings in my domain; nothing unusual about that. But the interesting thing is that the value of a property could be increased not with the addition of more buildings but rather with the construction of an attic. The children cherished and knew the value of having a place to hide. The children also knew that if and when summoned to board a transport heading east, there would be no place to play games. Resigned to this fate, the game was always left behind by those listed for transport so it could be played by the others remaining.

The artwork, sketches, stories, and poems written by the children frequently depicted life in my world and often in the starkest reality. However, some of their work came not from their eyes but from their hearts, not from what they saw but from what they craved. Hence, many of their drawings, poems, and prose reflected their yearning to escape which is why there were so many sketches and writings of colorful butterflies fluttering high above into an azure sky and away from my granite ramparts. Their work also reflected reminiscences about how things once had been: pastoral homes set in green, rolling hills, horses grazing in pastures, verdant gardens, and flowerpots balanced on window sills.

But as I said, for the most part, their work depicted the bleak milieu in which they resided: drab barracks, crowds of people, policemen, guards, barred windows, the food line. Franta Bass wrote a poem about a small, sweet boy, perhaps much like himself, who strolled in a garden of roses and who was destined to die when the first bud bloomed. Like the boy of his poem, Franta Bass died at the age of fourteen.

I felt the death of every one of my people, as they were all a part of me, but it was so much harder to bear the death of a child. Yet how could it be otherwise? When a child dies…words are inadequate. With tens of thousands of people living within me at any given time, I sometimes became confused and lost track of them all, so I came to rely on the official records of the German Authority. Yet even with the Germans' fastidious dedication for accuracy, somehow the number of children was never clear. I know that at least 12,000 children entered my realm, and possibly, the number is as high as 15,000. That some died while with me, and almost all who were transported were murdered, is also clear. Up to 1,600 children were liberated, but like their adult counterparts, within two weeks from liberation, many died from typhus.

Despite all efforts made by the doctors, nurses, teachers, room leaders, families, and almost every one of my people to spare them so that after the war they might find a future for themselves, at least nine out of ten children never reached adulthood. In the Paradise Ghetto and showcase to the world to demonstrate how well the Germans treated the Jews, almost all the children were annihilated—their present, their futures, and their lives cruelly stolen.

CHAPTER EIGHT: LIFE GOES ON

Not a mortal myself, though I am made from stuff which is human enough, I can only speak from what I learned from the way my people conducted themselves while struggling to remain alive. And although there were selfish and even heinous acts carried out by some of the inmates from time to time, for the most part, daily life was carried on in a most civil and even mundane manner—much to my amazement and admiration.

Of course, sometimes this arose from necessity rather than choice, such as the need to offer medical services. In the beginning, it was a daunting challenge to provide even a semblance of health care, something Dr. Erich Munk discovered upon arriving in my realm along with fourteen other physicians. Munk, who was appointed to head the health services, had to start quite literally from the ground (or beds, if you will) up. Upon learning there were no beds, the proud, meticulous, and quick-witted doctor who effused an aura of boundless energy and capacity to work, marched himself to head-quarters and, for what would be one of many times during his tenure, made a demand upon Edelstein and the Council for medical supplies. On that occasion, it was beds for his patients!

"What do you expect my patients to lie on?" Munk rhetorically asked Edelstein, whose forehead furrowed in response. "The floor? Propped up in the hallways?" Edelstein pushed his black-frame glasses up the bridge of his nose. Soon after, beds were delivered that had been reallocated from elsewhere; then followed the matter of sheets for the mattresses which was solved with contributions from other inmates. The first operation was an amputation conducted in a bathroom with the doctor using a carpenter's saw.

Despite the constant struggle for supplies, the quality of medical care equaled or even surpassed that of the major cities in Europe. The proficiency of the physicians was exceptional, and gradually, equipment and provisions began to trickle in, though not infrequently by surreptitious means. At the helm of the medical staff along with Munk was Professor Hermann Strauss who formerly served as director of the Jewish Hospital in Berlin. The health care system was organized in divisions describing their functions, such as home for newborns, old and sick people's care, blind, disabled, deaf and dumb, home for toddlers, and so on.

Outpatient clinics were established such as the one quartered in the Magdeburg barracks. Located on the first floor, the three rooms were subdivided by linen cloths strung up and dangling from the ceiling, demarcating different departments. Three dental chairs filled one area; across from that was a chaise longue equipped with the mystifying levers and rails of a radiation machine. In another section, the ophthalmology department was situated, consisting of a vision chart attached to a tottering cabinet. Low on the totem pole was the ear, nose, and throat division confined to a cramped space near the door. An overwhelmed dermatologist worked by a window, judiciously applying the limited amount of ointments he had on hand to serve the throngs of those suffering from a myriad of skin ailments so easily contracted in my environs. A large locker contained what medicine existed to fill preciously sought prescriptions.

I had already mentioned how special efforts were made to protect the young ones, and nowhere was this more apparent than in the children's hospital where as many as 100 children were housed and cared for by three doctors and a staff of thirty nurses. Everything was kept clean, and the youngest were bathed daily. Each room had white beds. While the older children played games such as chess, the staff kept the younger children occupied. Weather permitting, the youngsters were led outside into the well maintained gardens where they could stroll or sit and talk to each other. Frequently, tea and condiments were served in the afternoon.

The battle against infectious diseases such as typhus and the effort to avoid lice were waged by a committed team of physicians and their aides. How they held up under the pressure is beyond my comprehension. Sometimes, it was a matter of finding solace in other activities, which worked for Dr. Karl Fleischmann, who, at one time, supervised the entire health care system and was directly responsible for the treatment of 10,000 elderly people. His passions were poetry, painting, and literature, and through the medium of charcoal sketches, he portrayed my milieu. He often spoke about literature and recited poetry as part of the on-going lecture series.

One of the more memorable members of the medical staff was Viktor Frankl, an Austrian neurologist and psychiatrist who marched under my archways on September 25, 1942 accompanied by his wife and parents. Frankl had thick, dark hair combed back and bushy eyebrows that peeked over his eyeglasses. But his slight frame was no match for the day he spent in the Little Fortress where, after a thrashing, he was left with thirty-one flesh wounds. Recovering in his barracks and tended to by a nurse, he was uplifted by hearing a jazz band outside his window playing *Bei mir bist du schon (To me you are beautiful),* the unofficial anthem of my citizens.

Undeterred by the beating he received, Frankl served as a general practitioner in one of the clinics; later, relying on his expertise as a psychiatrist, he worked in the psychiatric care ward where he established a special clinic for newcomers and created a suicide watch for inmates suffering from despondency, a condition not unexpected given the conditions in which the people lived and the constant anxiety over the transports. Indeed, the number of suicides was considerably lower than I would have anticipated with 768 attempts and 246 "successful" in the first two years. Frankl reached out to the general populace by participating in the lecture series where he spoke not infrequently and began to lay the foundations of logotherapy, a school of psychiatry that no doubt was influenced by his time spent with me.

On October 16, 1944, along with his mother and wife—his father having died from pneumonia—Frankl was transported to Auschwitz where his mother was killed. His wife was subsequently murdered in Bergen-Belsen, but Frankl was liberated at Dachau.

In order to endure in my orbit—a world turned upside down—more than surviving the physical challenges was required; there was also the question of overcoming the spiritual and mental stresses. Some, like Frankl, sought out new paradigms to bring meaning into their lives; others relied on the arts and culture; and for many, it became a question of trusting in the core belief and heritage which landed them with me in the first place—their religion.

In my world, accommodations had to be made when it came to religious practice. Observing the commandment to honor the Sabbath was impossible; work was required, and there was no day of resting. Furtive services, however, were conducted out of sight of the German Authority. In attics, alleyways, and darkened rooms, people joined together and in hushed voices recited the liturgy for the holy day. Even the holidays presented a challenge. The first Yom Kippur in 1942 was officially a normal work day, but many of the inmates, especially the elderly, fasted even without the sustenance generally derived from the traditional large meal before the annual fast.

Two years later, the high holidays were observed more openly. Throughout my realm, in the largest halls and in the tiniest attics, people gathered for one hour of prayer in the early dawn before reporting for work; rooms that typically were adequate for the regular Sabbath service were now filled with people spilling over into the corridors. Nor was there a lack of rabbis to officiate the services, nor cantors to chant the prayers, nor choirs to sing the melodious tunes that lifted the spirits of the people.

At the end of the day, a dignified celebration was held in the largest dining room packed with 2,000 of my residents. After an organ recital, Dr. Epstein, then the head of the Council of Elders, exhorted the crowd with a theme that was more practical than spiritual. To survive, he said, we must be disciplined; each and every one of you must apply yourself to the work at hand; we will only survive with the strongest work ethic.

And what would religious life be without adherence to the laws, the *mitzvot* of the Torah? From the beginning, there was a rabbinical court headed by Rabbi Siegmund Unger, who was aided by two deputy rabbis. Hundreds of marriages were performed under the traditional wedding canopy—defiant avowals of love in a world plagued by hatred, resolute affirmations of life in the face of death. Indeed, etched forever in my memory are the beaming faces of many a young man and his betrothed, their eyes fixed upon one another, mirroring the love they shared. But on closer examination, tiny tears could be detected in the corners of their eyes, conceding the fact that in a day or two, sometimes even only hours, the newly wedded couple was scheduled for transport east, meaning inevitable separation and likely death.

There were other ways my people made me proud as they continually sought to create an environment more reminiscent of the world they had not long ago inhabited than evocative of the world in which they found themselves. And to accomplish this goal, what better way than carving out islands of time and space where the mind could be set free to swim like a fish in seemingly endless open waters.

In recognition of this craving the people held for the arts and cultural activities, only months after the arrival of my first occupants, the Council formally adopted the pursuit of leisure-time activities. At first, these programs were covertly conducted for fear the sounds of musical instruments or the reverberating of melodic voices might be overheard by the non-Jewish population of the ghetto, but when the last of those who had once called my spot on earth their home departed, there was a greater sense of ease in carrying out these activities, though great care still remained to stay out of sight of a passing German guard or officer. Consequently, to camouflage the functions of those organizing these activities, a young rabbi, Erich Weiner, was appointed director of what officially appeared to be religious events. There were even times when applause was forbidden to avoid attracting attention, but the performers and speakers could easily tell by the glowing faces and shining eyes of the audience how much they were appreciated.

In time, there was a greater openness in conducting the cultural activities as the German Authority adopted a pragmatic attitude, thinking: Might as well let the Jews play while they are here; one way or another, they'll all be dead.

Most performances were carried out in makeshift attics since there was little space under roof to be found anywhere else. Although plays were performed and lectures given, cabaret was the most popular form of theater—anything standing a chance to bring a smile or engender a chuckle, perhaps even a hearty belly laugh, was eagerly sought. Jokes relying on ghetto humor abounded. One of my favorites that became popular had to do with the upcoming visit of the Red Cross in '44 and reflected the pessimistic expectations held by the populace: All the fleas will be painted with phosphorous so that the commission will think they're fireflies. Sadly, this proved true.

Sometimes, however, there was concern a program might go too far, and no one dared to risk offending a passing German who, with nothing better to do, might stick his head inside to witness an event. Thus, *The Last Cyclist,* a satire by Karel Švenk, who had heralded a new brand of ghetto parodies that became popular, was banned by the Council of Elders because of its premise that a country governed by a dictator who outlawed all cyclists, blaming them for the nation's troubles, was far too close to Germany for the comfort of the Council.

Švenk objected vigorously. Raising his thick, black eyebrows and flashing his dark eyes at the Council members, he protested that the people were entitled to vent their anger at their oppressors in at least this relatively harmless way. But the injunction stood. Pursing his thin lips, Švenk accepted the decision; he had, after all, no other choice, just as he had no choice months later when he was deported to Auschwitz and following that, to a labor camp in Germany where he died.

Despite, and possibly because of, my people's vivid visions of flames swirling brightly into the black canopy of a night sky, fueled by blazing books pilfered from their homes, schools, libraries, and synagogues not all that long ago, the establishment of a library was paramount in their hearts. Thus, by late 1942, a library was opened, and within a year, it held 50,000 books, a fifth of which were in Hebrew and another fifth having to do with Zionism. Above the library was a small artists' studio where the painters Otto Ungar, Fritta Taussig, Peter Kien, and Leo Haas clandestinely drew a running chronicle of life within my walls. I shall speak more about these brave men later.

Because there was limited space, only those with a particular interest could actually visit the library. Consequently, a mobile library consisting of books in cardboard boxes made its way from building to building to deliver tomes specifically requested or to provide an opportunity for people to peruse the titles. None of this was much of a surprise to me; after all, these were the people of the book!

Given this limited access to the cherished tomes and the people's voracious appetite to read, to learn, to be entertained, and to be engaged, a fertile soil was propagated for the planting and growing of a vibrant cultural life. Oddly enough, the seeds for these activities were sown in the unlikeliest of places: the Orientation Service, whose job it was to assist inmates in finding their way about my environs. Later renamed the Auxiliary Service of the Ghetto Watch, these uniformed, mostly middle-aged men assumed assigned positions at various locations or traversed the cobbled streets and sidewalks, almost always with a touch of pomp and circumstance but also with an eagerness to help. These sober-minded men would offer their assistance to the confused and dazed newcomers or the elderly who couldn't remember where they were heading. Slowly, the sentinel would enunciate the directions or information required or if need be, take the befuddled person by the elbow and lead him or her to the proper destination.

Philip Manes was a member of this force. Manes, of whom I have spoken previously, was a man who maintained an unfailing ability to believe almost everything the German Authority asked the Jews to accept as true, even the currency bills they issued consisting of seven denominations ranging from one crown to 100 crowns with each printed in different colors. Manes had no hesitancy in accepting the value of these notes emblazoned with the visage of a hawk-nosed Moses staring out from the face of the bill, his forehead creased in evil contemplation and his side curls touching the tablets that he held aside his left ear. Of course, like so much in my realm, the currency was a façade. Indeed, the money was utterly worthless and could buy absolutely nothing, merely one more ruse crafted by the German Authority.

Despite this flaw in Manes's character, he contributed a great deal to enhance the quality of life of the people. Assuming command of the Auxiliary Service after the general police took over the task of assisting wayward denizens, Manes put his men to work organizing and producing cultural events including theatrical productions and adult education. The lecture series, which was generally held daily, stood out. This program was so popular that people had to sign up in advance to secure a seat in the audience since the demand often exceeded the availability of space. But upon looking at the dejected faces and shoulders slumped in resignation of those arriving after the room was filled, Manes and his men didn't have the heart to turn anyone away so people were permitted to stand in the aisles or at the rear or squeeze into a corner or nook, barely leaving room to breathe.

Speakers were never hard to secure; my population held a disproportionate number of learned men and women educated in a wide range of fascinating subjects. One of the first, Ludwig Sochaczewer, was discovered by Manes, standing helplessly with his plate at lunchtime. Manes immediately invited the stocky young man to share his encounters from when he had been a journalist. The stories he colorfully related from all parts of Europe had the audience leaning forward on the edges of their chairs. Louis Treumann, the distinguished Viennese operetta tenor, was another who captivated the audience as he spoke freely about his experiences, but ironically, he could not bring himself to sing.

Likely the most prominent and highly regarded speaker was Dr. Leo Baeck, the former spiritual leader of German Jewry who became the spiritual leader of the populace. When he spoke, it was as if a spell had been cast upon those in attendance; his easy-going demeanor and quiet calm conveyed the content convincingly. By contrast in style, the former Chief Rabbi of Berlin, Dr. Leopold Neuhaus, utilized his thickset frame and expressive eyes to rouse the audience, orating like a Hasidic rebbe vividly bringing to life the history of Jews and Judaism.

The people relished each event as if it might be the last because, after all, it could well be. Who knew what lay in store for anyone in the room? Disappointments were many in this regard. Dr. Judah Magnus, the eminent lawyer devoted to Jewry, was seventy-four when he delivered the first in what was to be a series of six lectures. His appearance was deceptive; dressed in a shabby overcoat with specks of food caught in his unruly beard, the old man displayed an energetic demeanor and unerring memory in his delivery. But before he could give the second lecture, he grew weaker and was transferred to the infirmary where Manes paid him a visit. Magnus had been struck by pneumonia and lay in bed with his eyes closed. Manes cleared his throat, and the eyes of the old man in the bed fluttered.

"Ah, Mr. Manes, what is new with you?"

"I am studying *Urfaust*," Manes replied.

"Ah, *Urfaust*...I would like to give a lecture on that. Beautiful, beautiful, *Urfaust*—fine." The next day, Magnus died.

On the eve of the 400th lecture, Manes was presented with a gift in acknowledgement of his singular contribution, a present which he earnestly accepted. With great care and fanfare, he deliberately unwrapped his treasure—a half loaf of bread, onions, and garlic. All in all, Manes produced over 500 events until his deportation to Auschwitz.

But do not take this to mean the only cultural events were those organized by the Auxiliary Service—quite the contrary! For example, from my first days, the members of the Women's International Zionist Organization from Brünn began meeting in small groups of twenty or so, usually on Saturday afternoons, for discussions. These activities were expanded in 1943 to include formal lectures, Hebrew studies, and gardening.

In an attic of the Magdeburg barracks, buzzing could be heard coming from the corners of the spaces where people gathered in tiny clusters. Someone might give a talk about Einstein's theory of relativity; another would lecture on the Middle Ages in Norway; people would be entranced by a lecture on Greek mythology; a lively debate usually followed a discourse about pre-Communist Russia. The cacophony was diverse with people speaking different languages and dialects, but the air and the tone shared a common element of life being breathed into my essence.

Of course poetry was recited in numerous venues, some formal and some not. Despite the fact there was always a high number of poets among my people, many having penned hundreds of poems, one poem that stands out in my mind was composed by Pavel Friedman, a young man who was a member of the youth movement Hehalutz, whose members lived and worked together. Pavel was often teased about his prominent nose and two left hands that made him all thumbs when it came to many of the tasks he was required to perform. But he more than made up for this with a boundless sensitivity which he readily shared with his companions. One night, he read a new poem he composed about a butterfly he had seen; in it he described its bright colors as it unfolded its wings and soared into the sky. But, he wrote, this had been the last butterfly he had seen since no butterfly lives in the ghetto any longer. Nor was it likely that Pavel would ever again see another butterfly because shortly thereafter, he was deported to Auschwitz where he died.

Who is to say what lifts the soul? Surely poetry, recitals, lectures, and theater possess that possibility, each serving, in one way or another, to ameliorate the misery induced by the environment the Germans created. Yet it was music that stood out in terms of reaching the most people and stirring their fondest memories. Perhaps this is so because music, in addition to its pleasing resonance, has a powerful ability to resurrect bygone times; also, it may be because music is international in its scope, and one performance can appeal to all of my people. Even the Germans, who attended on occasion, saw an ancillary advantage, using it for propaganda purposes. Consequently, operas, concerts, and even theater were often sanctioned by the German Authority.

In any event, from my earliest days, melodic sounds emanating from a vast array of sources permeated the air. A café orchestra was permitted by the Germans to impress any outside visitors; the Theresienstadt Symphony was established; the inmates were allowed to own musical instruments. People could stroll or sit on a bench or stretch out on the lawn to listen to the music played in the park. Sometimes groups gathered on the grass-covered roof of the Jaeger barracks, sat cross-legged or even laid on blankets to be entertained by musicians; in the evening, a trio might perform in the courtyard of the Dresdner barracks.

Do not think for a minute, however, that this was haphazard and spontaneous. Of course, there was always the occasion when someone playing only for himself on his instrument soon was surrounded by a small audience, and then another musician or two or a singer might join in. But most musical events were precisely planned by divisions that had been established in the cultural department to provide for chamber music, vocal music, and light music. There was a varied fare to appeal to any palate:

Kaff playing Chopin, Weiss's jazz quartet, the Ghetto Swingers troupe, Meyer and Santel's piano duo, Fircher's Liturgical Choir, performances of *The Marriage of Figaro*, *The Kiss*, and *Carmen*. But most memorable, likely because of the great effort made by the people behind them and the thousands of my residents who benefited, were the performances of *Brundibár*, *The Bartered Bride*, and *Requiem*.

Brundibár was spawned in Prague but matured in my realm where its progenitor, Hans Krása, had been sent. Krása was only half Jewish, his father being a Czech and his mother a German Jew, but this was enough to qualify him for residence within my walls. Growing up, he had been a student of the piano and violin, but his real success was as a composer. His last work before his arrest and deportation in August 1942 was *Brundibár*, a children's opera based on the play by Aristophanes.

I was impressed the moment I saw Krása after he made the trek from the train station and tramped under my archway. His thick, wavy hair was distinctly parted on the left. A broad Roman nose rested between deep-set eyes under luxuriant eyebrows. His face could have been carved out of granite and delivered a message that though he had been whisked away from the world he loved, he would not allow himself to be deprived of his ability to create. And though he remained productive for the two years he was with me, composing and producing chamber works often with fellow composers, it was his reworking of *Brundibár* that gave him the greatest satisfaction. Indeed, the Germans were so impressed that a performance was filmed and included in the footage comprising the German propaganda film "Hitler Gives the Jews a City." For this, the composer was rewarded with a one-way ticket to Auschwitz where, at the age of forty-five, he was murdered.

Among the earliest of my denizens was Heddi Grabouc who organized the women in her barracks to perform musicals. In doing so, she sought the talents of Rafi Schächter, a small man in his thirties with pitch black hair. Together, they conducted rehearsals in the freezing cellar, and arising from this venue, many concerts were held including *The Marriage of Figaro*, *The Kiss*, and most notably, *The Bartered Bride*, which was performed thirty-five times and premiered on November 28, 1942.

The musicians for *The Bartered Bride* were organized and led by Karel Ančerl, who had arrived in my domain only weeks before the premiere with his wife Valy and young son Jan. Ančerl was quite noticeable as he strutted through my gates. He was a distinguished-looking man with his thick hair combed back, prominent nose, and a cleft on his jutting chin. Though only thirty-four, he had already been held in high esteem in Prague, and he soon became the leader of the string orchestra.

On more than one occasion, Ančerl would gaze out at the audience while conducting the musicians. He would consider the faces staring back—of sick, old, starving people—and he marveled how their expressions were transformed into visages of contentment and pleasure. This led him to contemplate the power of music, and he concluded that the sway music held was so great that it drew every human being possessing a heart and open mind into its realm, enabling one to bear the hardest hours of life. For most of my people, those hardest hours were endured in my domain.

Ančerl's final performance in October 1944 was conducting the string orchestra as part of the German propaganda movie. Balancing himself on a flimsy wooden platform, he conducted a work by Pavel Haas, also an inmate, as children sang standing behind flower pots so their bare feet would not be noticed. After the filming was complete, as recompense, Ančerl, his wife, and son, along with Haas and others involved in the production, were sent to Auschwitz. Ančerl survived; Valy and Jan died in the gas chambers.

In 1943, 413 theatrical productions were performed within my walls. The crowning musical event that year was Verdi's *Requiem*, but this was only achieved after overcoming almost insurmountable impediments, calling for a fierce determination to succeed. This was largely accomplished through the efforts of one man, Rafael Schächter, the conductor.

Schächter knew from the beginning what he wanted to serve as the pinnacle of that year's artistic efforts, but *Requiem* was far from a unanimous choice, and it carried potentially lethal risks. Many were hesitant about daring to perform the Roman Catholic mass for the dead inside a Jewish ghetto under the omniscient surveillance of the German Authority. Why not one of Handel's three Jewish oratorio, instead? Wouldn't this make more sense? Be more prudent? Many suggested so.

But Schächter remained adamant. Just because we are compelled to live in a place that challenges every aspect of a civilized society does not mean we should give up striving for a share in humanity's cultural heritage, he argued. Ultimately, Schächter prevailed, although the path to performing *Requiem* had fateful twists and turns. Yet somehow, the premiere was scheduled and not only with the permission of the Germans but actually with their blessing. After all, the Germans reminded their prisoners, were the Germans not a sophisticated people whose appreciation for culture and beauty was without peer?

For the premiere, the cast was to be honored with the presence of SS Lieutenant Colonel Adolf Eichmann, who always took a perverted pleasure in seeing his vision of what I was to become realized. Taking a seat at the front, he squared his shoulders and braced his slight frame, removing the officer's hat that covered so much of his prominent forehead. His hawkish nose screwed up as it prepared to snort in disdain at the remotest suggestion he was merely one of the audience in attendance while his thin lips twisted a smirk in anticipation of what the parasitic Jewish performers could produce.

But as the event went on and the four star soloists backed by a chorus of 150 men and women brought home the beauty and pathos of the funeral hymn, the certitude on Eichmann's face gradually gave way to bewilderment; he lost his smug demeanor; at times, he even appeared moved into a wistful reverie as the Jewish inmates created an angelic, mournful beauty in this hell on earth Eichmann had hatched.

Appropriately enough, as a reward for this premier performance, mass deportations were ordered, dispatching 5,000 souls to Auschwitz; included in this convoy were most of the members of *Requiem*'s chorus. But Schächter would not be deterred, and although his troupe would be similarly sheared of its members on two more occasions, new people would be recruited and trained, and the concerts continued.

I have no doubt that *Requiem* and the countless other performances contributed to the well-being of my people. Indeed, I would argue that lives were literally saved because of it. For example, there was Mariánka Zadikow, a young woman of twenty when she participated in *Requiem*. Her father, Arnold, was a noted sculptor and portraitist who sculpted a model of my domain which proved to be his last home on earth when he died from a ruptured appendix. Mariánka's mother, Hilda, was a skillful painter who, during the early morning hours, painted in pursuit of her passion but otherwise was on-call to utilize her skills to benefit the Germans for whom she designed coats of arms for glove boxes and book covers.

As for Mariánka, each time she participated in a performance of *Requiem*, her spirits were lifted as she gazed at the audience and saw a room filled with emaciated, lonely people, many old and sick, briefly transformed into individuals with relaxed countenances bearing occasional smiles and even teary eyes; people who, for an hour and a half, had glimpses of their pasts where they had once been happy. Taking this in,

Mariánka could not help but think to herself that this was because of the music she and the others were performing—the music the audience had once enjoyed and now from which they were once again deriving pleasure. Perhaps some would manage to survive because of this, Mariánka pondered. Just as I have, she considered further. "Me…I am a survivor because of *Requiem*."

L'chayim is the Jewish toast to life. Each day, every day, every hour of every day, and every moment that was imbued with one of my people performing one act—tending to a young child with fever, applying bandages to an open wound, joining a *minyan* to satisfy the requisite number of ten to hold a prayer service, raising a question in a spirited discussion over a book, lecturing to an eager audience with an insatiable thirst for knowledge, joining the chorus in an operetta, playing a musical instrument for passersby to hear. Anything to make my milieu seem ordinary and safe, just as their lives had once been in another time and in another world; anything to belie the awful truth that behind the façade that was created lay a reality too terrible to acknowledge or comprehend, or even worse, to surrender to.

CHAPTER NINE: THE RED CROSS VISIT

Like every proud father, my *paterfamilias*, the blond-haired Aryan whose towering presence stood in stark contrast to his high-pitched voice, SS Obergruppen-führer Reinhard Heydrich, held a vision for his offspring that I would become the showplace to the world proving how well the Führer treated the Jews. Yet, almost from the beginning, there were those who were wary of this brazen claim. Not that there was much concern about the way Jews fared under the ever-widening noose the Third Reich had looped over Europe; it was more a matter of catching Herr Hitler in a lie so he could be embarrassed—a public relations gambit supporting the Allied depiction of the conflict as good versus evil. But make no mistake; very few people and certainly no government went out of the way to rescue the Jews from their fate.

Hence, from the announcement of my birth, suspicious voices were raised about how the Jews would manage in this new utopian city established by the Nazis for the benefit of this forlorn race. There were even some who began asking for an inspection by the International Red Cross. By the time of the first anniversary marking the official opening of my gates, the World Jewish Congress formally requested that the International Red Cross address the conditions within my walls. In response, the German Red Cross stated quite matter-of-factly that everything was fine, and there was nothing to be done. Not wishing to risk a diplomatic flare-up and make matters worse, the International Red Cross decided against lodging an official complaint or pursuing the matter further, thereby setting a dangerous precedent which would be followed repeatedly by organizations and governments in the months and years to come.

More than anything, it was this sense of fear that challenging or questioning the claims made by the Nazi regime—no matter how absurd and unbelievable they might be—would only exacerbate the problem, a theme repeated over and over around the globe so that in the end, six million Jews were murdered with barely an outcry until it was a *fait accompli*. What could these people have been thinking? How much worse could matters have progressed than they already had amidst the silence the world proffered in response to the German solution of the Jewish problem!

Unfortunately, the Germans were proficient at many things, and at the top of the list was propaganda. Goebbels was a genius, and his staff expertly and efficiently executed his directives with precise effectiveness. In May 1943, journalists (German journalists, of course) were welcomed into my domain to give credence to the claim that I was nothing less than a remarkable oasis in a war-ravaged continent. The compliant reporters carefully focused their eyes in the direction to which they were pointed by their congenial escorts who, with puffed chests and arms waving in the air, shepherded the entourage on their tour: a tour of the housing of the prominents, a most professional and entertaining theater performance, an inspection of the bank—the center of healthy commerce—where the fictitious currency could personally be handled, and finally, a walk through the courthouse where Jews dispensed justice to other Jews. Anticipating that journalists would be journalists (even German journalists) and the possibility that inquiries might be made, the inmates were instructed not to answer any questions if asked. Instead, simply smile, pretend not to understand, nod in ignorance, or better yet, happily walk away; just do not answer questions. And everyone knew better than not to comply.

His confidence bolstered from the successful visit by the German journalists, Eichmann personally escorted two members of the German Red Cross through my realm the following month. But this did not go as well as anticipated. Despite the same camouflage and trickery employed only weeks before, the representatives concluded that medical services were inadequate and living conditions were disgraceful. Learning of the report, Eichmann seethed as beads of perspiration burst across his protruding forehead. Pushing his black-framed glasses over the bridge of his hawkish nose, he quietly but firmly resolved this would never happen again. There would be no more visits by any Red Cross officials—at least not until proper preparations were made to deceive anyone and everyone, he determined.

Ironically, it was the Germans themselves who created the circumstances that resulted in insurmountable pressure for another Red Cross inspection. This arose from a decision made in October 1943 to relocate 466 Danish Jews to my realm, a miniscule number representing barely 0.3% of my total population. But unlike the rest of the world, the Danish government, emboldened by King Christian X, cared about its Jews, and he insisted on being informed about the condition of his citizens. Ultimately, the Germans had no choice but to acquiesce to the demands for an inspection by the International Red Cross. There was no avoiding it, but contrived delays did succeed in buying precious time for the Germans to fabricate an illusory domain.

The first task in need of attention was to eliminate the overcrowding. For this, the solution was simple and obvious—more transports east killing more Jews. Beginning in the fall of '43 and continuing right up until May of the following spring, over 17,000 of my people were sent to Auschwitz/Birkenau where most were greeted by immediate death. However, unlike in the past, those assigned to the transports were assiduously selected by the Germans to accomplish another purpose: cleanse my milieu of occupants who might give the Red Cross inspectors pause. Those suffering from tuberculosis were promptly placed at the top of the transport list followed by disheveled orphans whose deadened eyes gazed forlornly out of their gritty faces. On the other hand, those who looked relatively healthy, and especially girls with the potential to become pretty, rosy-cheeked young maidens prancing over my cobblestone streets, were kept off the lists.

The other thing that had to be accomplished was to replace the brutish Anton Burger with a suave and sophisticated commandant who was capable of putting on an air of charm and civility for the international community. Such a man was Karl Rahm, whose erect posture, polished demeanor, and self-possessed stare inspired confidence and trust. Rahm was also a technician by profession and thus, someone inclined to immerse himself in the details and minutiae of my refurbishing as I was transformed to display a world so pleasant and credible that one could never imagine the truth behind my veneer.

What became known as the beautification program began in earnest in April 1944. Appropriately enough, it was spring, and while the sun shone brightly in the sky and the daylight hours extended, a strong, cold wind still whipped its way through the streets and alleys of my domain causing those outdoors to clutch their frayed outerwear to their skeletal bodies and tilt their faces downward from the blustery blasts. The trees had yet to begin their recovery from the winter, and they grotesquely encircled the parade ground with their bald, broom-like branches. In quick time, both the weather and my milieu would be altered dramatically.

The overhaul began outside my bulwarks. Initially, those destined to inhabit my realm had a considerable walk from the Bauschowitz train station. Subsequently, however, railway lines were laid by the inmates all the way to my ramparts, and the Bauschowitz Gate was established, allowing trains to pass through my outer walls. While the Germans claimed this was undertaken out of humanitarian concerns to make travel easier and more efficient, I suspect the real motivation was to keep prying eyes from observing Jews boarding transports headed east. In any event, anticipating the arrival of the Red Cross inspectors, a wall of green turf was constructed in place of the menacing protective casements marking my exterior, which would have been the first impression perceived by a visiting delegation, and the inmates were encouraged to plant vegetable gardens on the grounds between the moat and the walls.

Inside my fortification, renovations were carried out feverishly. The main square, which in the winter had served as a big tent for the packaging production, was converted into a garden. A music pavilion was erected at the south side of the square across from a café. The great park that had been closed for two years was reopened, and almost overnight, grass grew, dense foliage swathed the grounds, and sandpits appeared for the children. Saplings were planted around the barracks. Beds of greenery emerged everywhere, and benches were placed at entryways.

Planks and barbed wire that had closed off streets were removed. Everything was open and free, leaving no signs of captivity. Sidewalks were scrubbed. Buildings that looked dilapidated were repaired. Like worker bees building a beehive, people were buzzing about everywhere, filling holes with plaster, painting ceilings and walls, and cleaning and scrubbing exposed surfaces to the rigorous standards of the exacting Germans. A modern children's home was built of wood and glass and supplied with new beds, showers, and even a playground and swimming pool. All the residences along the anticipated route which the inspectors would take were whitewashed and fitted with flower boxes. To make the living quarters appear less crowded, the third tier of the bunks on the ground floors were cut down.

Special attention was paid to the residences of the prominents and specific community buildings. The hospital was issued fresh linens, and the nurses were given pristine new uniforms. Street numbers were replaced by names, such as Lake Street,

Mountain Street, and Hunter Street. And as if there were not enough rules to violate, which often meant transport east, additional regulations were promulgated, such as banning laundry from hanging out of windows and prohibiting the disabled to leave their quarters, all to bolster the chimera that I was a wonderful place for Jews to live. Finally, after intense pressure, the Germans could delay no longer, and Himmler acquiesced to a visit by the International Red Cross in June. Let the show go on!

On June 23, 1944, the long-anticipated inspection by the International Red Cross took place. The mission was to determine whether there was any validity to the rumors, accusations, and reports that Germans were responsible for the deaths of tens of thousands of Jews. This was to be resolved by the unfettered scrutiny of my domain and the residents.

Naturally, I was honored to be selected for such an important role. But this is not to say I was without misgivings. Like an actor on a stage, I was outfitted in a costume to which I was not accustomed—indeed, it was the antithesis of my normal attire. Would I be recognized for what I was or for something I was not? And if the latter, was there any harm? Do not most audiences seek a respite from reality, to be transported to a fantasy realm, and is this not the performer's mission? After all, there was only to be one performance to last no more than six hours for the official inspectors to observe an entire city and its thousands of inhabitants. How naïve for anyone, let alone diligent investigators, to think that amount of time would be sufficient to pierce any pretense and perceive the reality beyond. As I said, I had my misgivings.

The curtain was raised on a fine summer day with an unusually translucent blue sky; the sun shined brightly, easily sliding its way in an arch across the expansive firmament. Suddenly, almost out of nowhere, the official entourage of three appeared. In the forefront was Dr. Franz Hvass, a representative of the Danish Foreign Office, followed by Dr. Yuel Henningsen, representing the Danish health commissioner on behalf of the Danish Red Cross, and Dr. Maurice Rossel of the Swiss Red Cross. Surrounding the delegation and slinking along like a gelatinous amoeba were Gestapo officials and representatives of the German Foreign Office, all accoutered in civilian attire.

With due pomp and circumstance, the delegation was formally greeted by the head of the Council. Standing stiffly in a black suit with his starched collar stifling his neck and wearing a top hat, Dr. Paul Epstein offered an introduction to the lovely town of Theresienstadt including a recitation of specific facts and figures, none of which had anything to do with reality nor my true nature. When Epstein finished, he strode to a chauffeur-driven car and slid into the back seat, bumping into its current occupant. Lifting his head and uttering an apology, the leader of the Jewish Council trembled when he recognized the SS officer who, only the day before, had brutally kicked and beaten him.

The ensemble then embarked on the official inspection guided by the ever gracious and poised Commandant Rahm. Radiating an aura of confidence and geniality, Rahm led the delegation over spotless streets, past houses with windows dressed in bright pastel shades, and through an adorable Maria Theresa village. Not by coincidence, a group of female agricultural workers passed the legation as if by chance. With hoes on their shoulders and uplifted voices, they filled the air with joyous song. Along the way, several children ran up to the commandant, smiling and calling out "Uncle Rahm, Uncle Rahm," with one little lad tugging at the commandant's jacket, asking, "Uncle Rahm, are we getting sardines again?" Rahm laughed and brushed his fingers through the boy's hair, answering in the affirmative but looking at the delegates and not the boy as he did.

Just as the legation arrived at the soccer field, a goal was scored at that precise moment, exactly according to script. Reaching the community center, the Terezín orchestra played Mozart for the delegation. At the bank, the inspectors were allowed to handle the official paper currency supposedly used by the populace. The man in charge, Herr Director Friedmann, with his chest inflated in self-importance as he puffed profusely on a cigar, offered cigarettes to the visitors while he explained the importance of the bank in communal life. He went on and on about cash reserve and the monitoring of the currency's circulation, ignoring the fact that the whole thing was a complete fabrication, and the currency was utterly worthless.

There was a long and festive lunch where delicacies were served as if they were standard fare for the residents. An ensemble sang *Requiem*. How blind could the inspectors have been not to see the irony of emaciated Jews singing, "*Libera me, Domine, de morte Aeterna,*" meaning, "Deliver me, O Lord, from eternal death." By seven that evening, the visit had ended.

Before the inspection had been undertaken, Dr. Maurice Rossel, the Swiss representative, had his doubts and concerns, and he had prepared himself "for the worst," wondering why the Germans kept delaying the visit. But as the inspection wore on, he found himself astonished to discover that "the ghetto was a community leading an almost normal existence." He was impressed by how the food rations were similar to everyone else living in the Protectorate with the lone exception that margarine was substituted for butter. Rossel's official report sent to Eberhard von Thadden, the legislative councilor of the German Foreign Office, found conditions satisfactory and suggested that the visit will reassure many people concerned about the populace. The report made by the entire commission to the Red Cross in Stockholm was even more confounding; it was laudable, concluding I was anything but the filthy ghetto that some detractors had the audacity to suggest. Indeed, I was an oasis in war-ravished Europe providing a comfortable community for elderly Jews to live out their lives—just as Herr Hitler had promised.

Could this be true? Could Rossel and the others not have seen through the deception? Could they have been tricked so easily? Epstein believed not. He was convinced the commission was not duped. They saw through the façade. How could it be otherwise?

One of the delegates, Dr. Hvass, later claimed that their findings were pragmatic; they had exaggerated the praise deliberately so the Germans, who were known to respond angrily to criticism, would allow the Danes to continue to send food to their Jewish compatriots residing in my realm. But does this justify closing their eyes to the suffering of the vast majority of inmates who were not Danish Jews? Did Hvass care at all about the non-Danish Jews, or did he view them only somewhat more benignly than the Nazi portrayal of Jews as not being human? Was much convincing needed for Hvass and the others to see my inhabitants as a race of parasitic vermin just as the Germans had always claimed, and therefore, no matter how awful the conditions they were compelled to live under, it was better than they deserved?

As I have pondered these questions, and I have had more than enough time to do so, it is my belief that the Red Cross delegates replicated the feelings and attitudes of those who comprised the organizations they represented, which, in turn, was a manifestation of the countries and populations from which they came—in other words, the whole world. Who in his or her right mind for even a moment could possibly entertain the suggestion that my province was a wonderful place for Jews to thrive, which is what the Germans had the audacity to suggest. And this, no less, in the middle of 1944, after more than a decade of discrimination, persecution, expulsion, confinement, punishment, and methodical mass murder had been inflicted upon European Jewry, all of which was common knowledge to everyone by the time of the inspection, if not before. Those who made the report, studied the report, and accepted the report were either idiots or didn't care about the slaughter of the Jews, and in my estimation, it was more a matter of the latter than the former.

In any event, encouraged by the receptiveness to the notion I was a haven for Jews and an example of how much the Third Reich cared for this wretched and cursed people, the Germans decided to take the matter a step further and produce a propaganda film so the entire world could see what the Red Cross delegation had witnessed firsthand. After all, why waste the material and expenses making me appear so picturesque when they could serve as perfect props in a film? There was not a moment to lose. Arrangements commenced almost immediately after the Red Cross delegates rendered their findings. Once again, I was on the world stage and called upon to perform!

Rahm was more than up for the task. On a brilliant summer's day, he summoned Kurt Gerron to his office. Gerron was just the man for the job, Rahm concluded, perusing the inmate's background. Born in Germany to Jewish parents, he had become a stage actor after deciding medicine was not his calling, and by 1930, he was a director at a Berlin theater. He also directed movies, including Marlene Dietrich in *The Blue Angel*, a film that gained international acclaim, which Rahm knew well. The image of the star's nylon-sheathed legs stretched seductively over the sides of a high-backed chair had been permanently implanted in the commandant's mind's eye—a vision so foreign to the milieu in which Rahm now found himself. When Hitler came to power, Gerron fled Germany to France and then settled in Amsterdam where he continued making movies until he was arrested by the SS in 1943; soon after that, he was delivered to me.

"Herr Gerron," Rahm greeted the inmate entering his office. By addressing the prisoner with respect, it was obvious that Rahm was up to something, and he promptly proceeded to the matter at hand. "You will make a film about how wonderful life is here, and it shall be called *Der Führer schenkt den Juden eine Stadt*: *The Führer gives the Jews a City.*" Gerron was taken aback. But it was certainly not his place to question his task, only to carry it out. To do otherwise would likely mean death. But Gerron also saw an opportunity, and he seized upon it, extracting from Rahm a promise that in exchange for his work, he and his wife would not be sent east. But one cannot make a pact with the devil and expect honesty in dealings, can one? As it turned out, Gerron had merely bought himself some time; after completing the film the following month, he and his wife were dispatched to Auschwitz and murdered.

Rahm made it clear that there was no time to lose. Gerron conferred with the Council of Elders who supported his efforts since no one wanted to risk offending Rahm. With the help of a Berlin manufacturer who was also an amateur writer by the name of Greifenhagen, he set out to work on the script. By July, the script was complete, and a team of documentary cameramen arrived from Berlin.

One would expect that finding actors would not be a problem given the thousands living within my walls. Ironically, the opposite was true. Few Jews wanted to appear in the film despite the fact that their rations would be tripled to put some meat on their emaciated skeletons. But there were always people about, and once the cameras whirred, and the lights focused on the stunned prisoners, people calmly drifted in and out of sight, scuttling along the cobbled streets and ambling into alleyways.

A decree from Berlin that only inmates who looked Jewish should be filmed did not make matters any easier for Gerron and his troupe to fill out the cast. This meant filming persons with hooked noses, dark hair, and coal-black or brown eyes. Even better was to find those with stooped shoulders and twisted, satanic torsos propelling themselves forward on spindly legs, moving like spiders seeking out their hapless prey.

In a few instances, there was no leeway in casting, and only certain people could play themselves, such as in the case of the Council of Elders. But even here, there was more than enough room for deception. Indeed, the stage and setting were altered, as the cameras did not record the dingy, dilapidated room in the Magdeburg barracks where the Council actually met but instead focused the lenses on an airy, bright room in the gymnasium where a formally attired Epstein addressed his colleagues. Unbeknownst to Epstein, what he said was not recorded, and his speech would be dubbed back in Berlin.

Like the play presented for the Red Cross delegation, an illusory world was created. Firemen in new uniforms put out a fire; smiling children cavorted up a flight of stairs; a boy, no more than six or seven with short hair, grinned into the camera; a dark-eyed, Mediterranean-looking girl leisurely sipped from a cup with her face half hidden; Commandant Rahm, dressed spiffily in his uniform, welcomed a trainload of children from Holland, lifting youngsters from the wagons with a fatherly smile pasted on his face. But once the cameramen ceased shooting, and my world slipped back into its previous existence, and reality began to set in, these very same wide-eyed, carefree youngsters were placed on yet another train—but that one was bound for Auschwitz.

Oddly enough, *The Führer gives the Jews a City* was never shown. In fact, it was not even edited. Except for a few photos, there is no physical evidence that the film and the world it depicted ever even existed. Much like myself.

CHAPTER TEN: "THE PAINTERS' AFFAIR"

The Red Cross visit was a successful deception, as the Germans painted a panoramic portrait of what they wanted the world to see that was, for the most part, widely accepted. But for many months before that there were more than a few pairs of restless eyes seeing my world as it truly was and dutifully sketching quite different depictions entirely. When discovered by the Germans the month after the Red Cross delegation departed, those responsible were swiftly and mercilessly dealt with. Their story became known as The Painters' Affair, and this is how it happened.

As is sometimes said, beauty is in the eye of the beholder. So who is qualified to ascertain beauty, let alone determine who the ones to create it are? Nonetheless, by acceptable and traditional norms, among my people there were at least thirty-four professional artists and architects with designated duties plying their craft. Some of these people worked at the Lautsch Company producing decorative objects, ceramics, and paintings. Others were assigned to construct stage sets for productions and sketches for Nazi propaganda films. Still more worked out of several offices in the Magdeburg barracks and were charged with the task of preparing graphic illustrations of statistics and reports. What all these artists had in common was access to paper, canvas, oil brushes, and other supplies and tools which they surreptitiously utilized for their more clandestine artwork.

Most of these men were Czech, but there were some Germans, Dutch, and Austrians as well. The ones I best remember were the ringleaders of The Painters' Affair: Leo Haas, Bedrich Taussig (commonly known as Fritta), Felix Bloch, Otto

Ungar, and Norbert Troller. While a number of artists, such as the painter Dolfi Aussenberg and Dr. Teichman, created work designed to portray my true nature, they were fortunately not caught up in this most tragic set of circumstances. But alas, not so for the five men who were designated by the Germans as the instigators of horror propaganda.

Otto Ungar was born in 1901 and educated in Prague. He had taught painting, math, and geometry at a Jewish secondary school in Brno and had been a professor of design. By nature, Ungar was a quiet, reserved man with swarthy hair combed back above his head. His round, fleshy face and full lips lent a feminine aura to his mien, engendering a sanguine expression. But his cadaverous eyes and sullen stare bespoke something quite the opposite, exposing the pessimistic outlook entrenched within the man. Unger stood in stark contrast to the good humor and outgoing disposition of Dr. Fleischmann, a dermatologist, who painted and wrote poetry often portraying my true nature.

Another ringleader who found himself enmeshed in the German net was the head draftsman in the construction office, Bedrich Taussig, who was generally addressed by his pen name, Fritta. In Prague, Fritta had worked as an illustrator, a commercial artist, and a draftsman. When he reached my gates, he was accompanied by his wife and infant son, Thomas. For his boy, Fritta created children's books, each handmade in a limited edition of one original copy bound with coarse, brown cloth and filled with bright drawings and colorful captions written in large, neat lettering. To see such a book eagerly received with the innocent eyes of a child was an oasis in a wasteland of despair.

Sometimes the artists busied themselves creating artwork for my younger inhabitants while at other times, children served as the subjects for their work. The famous illustrator Leo Haas was quick to take advantage of the fact that next door to him lived the Klima family that included a nine-year-old boy named Ivan who was perfectly suited to model for his sketches. The lad was an ideal subject with his deep-set eyes and long eyebrows projecting a serous gaze and pointed ears standing in stark contrast to a tiny mouth. Ivan willingly obliged and was so fascinated watching Haas at his work that he asked for his own paper so he, too, could make drawings. At first reluctant to part with any of the scarce and precious commodity, Haas denied the request, but seeing the look of disappointment on Ivan's face, he recanted and provided the fledgling artist with a sheet on which the boy drew a lineup in the food court.

During the day, Fritta, Haas, Felix Bloch, Ungar and Norbert Troller, who hailed from a prominent Czech family of businessmen, though he himself was trained as an architect, were all kept busy drafting charts for the Germans, whose appetite was voracious for diagrams, maps, boxes, arrows, and chains of command. But when they were not at work, these men and others sketched and painted their impressions of my milieu as it truly existed, reflecting the hopelessness and misery they observed every minute of every hour, all of which was undertaken at great personal risk. Their work was kept hidden for its discovery by the Germans would no doubt be met with immediate transport east—or worse.

Almost all of the men's free time was devoted to this undertaking, sometimes eight to ten hours a day and almost every day of the week. Most of the time, they worked at night, but whenever the guards were absent or distracted, an artist or two would pull out a small sketch pad and hastily draw a portrait of reality. The leaders of the group, Haas and Fritta, encouraged the others to accurately illustrate conditions in my world with the phrase, "Write this down, Kisch," which was a Czech expression meaning, "Tell it like it is." Fritta, who had always been political and hated the Germans, drew pen-and-ink sketches depicting my people as a sea of hungry faces with eyes wide in terror and despair. Haas's drawings expressed a sense of outrage, reflecting his talent as a caricaturist and a political man.

While none of the men expected compensation for their efforts, some of their work was more commercial and brought them some recompense. For example, paintings were made of the bakers who fancied seeing themselves on canvas and rewarded the artists with extra loaves of bread. But allowing their creations to see the light of day was fraught with peril and bound to end badly. And indeed, this is how things came undone.

It began with František Strass who was a prolific customer of the sketches and paintings made by Fritta, Ungar, and the others. Strass was a man of seventy who formerly had been a department store owner and wealthy wholesale textile dealer who took an interest in the arts and became a collector. Because of his gentile family relations, Strass had special privileges, and through his connections with the Czech gendarmes, he was able to smuggle in contraband, such as cigarettes, food, and even money. This was not a one-way street. Strass was also able to smuggle items out, which he did with much of the artwork he purchased, even adding captions to some of the sketches.

Convinced that the paintings and drawings would be safe in Switzerland, Strass felt certain he could reclaim them after the war, but somehow, several of the sketches were printed in Swiss newspapers, and the Germans got wind of it. A Gestapo officer named Rudolf Haindl, infamous even by Nazi standards, was dispatched to my realm and ordered to quickly get to the bottom of the matter, put an end to such activities, and punish the perpetrators. Not only did he accomplish his task, but along the way, he was rewarded with the position of commandant of the Gestapo in my domain. Haindl had an insatiable appetite for sadism, and my people were the perfect fodder to fulfill his cravings.

One night soon after his arrival, Haindl ordered all the tuberculosis patients in the hospital to stand naked in the open doorways. Fits of coughing resonated off the walls; twisted torsos leaned against the doorframes for support; beads of feverish sweat burst on foreheads despite the frigid air. Many died that night while others who managed to make it through to the early dawn hours expired that much sooner because of Haindl's brutality. What chance did my artists have against such a villain?

How Haindl managed to get to the bottom of things occurred by chance. An inmate had asked Strass for a loan, which Strass refused, suspecting that the man was an agent provocateur. The man, who was never publicly identified, sent an anonymous note to Haindl denouncing Strass. Unannounced and to Strass's surprise, Haindl and his thugs barged into Strass's quarters and tore the place apart looking for anything and everything but nothing in particular. When ripping off the bed sheets and flinging the pillows into the air, several folders filled with sketches, some even having captions, were discovered. Then Haindl knew who smuggled the defamatory drawings from my realm.

Strass cowered under Haindl's thunderous recriminations. But that was not all. The sadist took pleasure in pummeling the elderly man first with his fists and then by kicking him. All the while, Strass lay rolled up in a ball on the floor, absorbing the blows as he moaned and pleaded for mercy. Eventually, Haindl grew weary, and he ceased the beating, taking time to catch his breath. There was no point in wasting his energy on the old Jew. The furious Gestapo commandant was more interested in apprehending the creators of the offensive contraband, not its purveyor.

Meanwhile, hearing that Strass had been taken into custody, Fritta and Haas carefully went about concealing their work. Haas pried open some paneling and secreted the sketches within a wall while Fritta located a large tin case in which he deposited many of his pictures. When he thought no one was looking, Fritta lugged the case through alleyways until he spotted a plot of ground used for farming, where he buried it. Of course, nothing could be done about the artwork that Strass had sent to Switzerland and by then was likely in the possession of the Germans. The only thing to do was wait and hope for the best.

Several weeks passed with nothing out of the ordinary occurring. Then, one day, rumor had it that several SS officers arrived. Shortly thereafter, Fritta, Haas, Felix Bloch, and Otto Ungar were summoned to the headquarters of the Jewish Council where they were ushered into the office of Dr. Otto Zucker, deputy to Epstein, the Council's head. Without much ado and barely looking up from his desk, Zucker spoke matter-of-factly, "Tomorrow morning, you are all to report to Commandant Rahm's office."

"What is this about?" Each man asked in one voice. Zucker shrugged; he did not know nor have any idea. "But I suggest you bring along a warm coat and warm underclothing," he offered.

"Why? It is summer," one of the men thought aloud.

"The cellar of the SS can get quite cold even now, I have heard." That alone made the men quake. "But even if you are detained for a while," Zucker added, trying to alleviate their anxiety, "I'm sure everything will turn out all right." He forced a smile and ushered them one by one out the door.

The following morning, July 16, 1944, the four men reported as instructed to the SS office where they were joined by Norbert Troller and František Strass. Troller, who was not forewarned about the possibility of being locked in the cellar, was accoutered in shorts and sandals, which were more appropriate to the day's oppressive heat. Unlike the others, who displayed only apprehensive expressions, Strass couldn't conceal the fear and panic in his eyes, having been previously beaten by Haindl. He alone had a foretaste of what would be in store for them. He also knew there was no denying his culpability, having been caught with his hand in the proverbial cookie jar since acquiring artwork was forbidden by the Germans, and they already had the goods on him for that much.

Although it was his office, in deference, Commandant Rahm stood off by the side, being outranked by some of the SS officers who were present: SS Captain Moes, known as the bird of death for his role supervising the final massacre at Bergen-Belsen; SS Captain Hans Günther, the chief SS officer in Prague; and no one other than Adolf

Eichmann himself, who sat quietly behind Rahm's desk. The War had taken a bit of a toll on Lieutenant Colonel Adolf Eichmann, head of the Jewish Office of the Gestapo's Internal Security Bureau. Eichmann's slight torso appeared almost emaciated as he sat unbending, his skin pallid, his eyes with an odd glitter while gazing off into a realm known only to himself.

The men remained standing in stupefied silence before Eichmann and his henchmen. Eichmann took a deep breath, pushed his black-frame glasses over the bridge of his nose, and commenced speaking in a tone reminiscent of a friendly conversation with a wayward acquaintance.

Gentlemen, he began, you must know by now how I have nothing but the most humane intentions concerning your people. Why, look around you at the wonderful place the Führer has provided—this fine city, Theresienstadt! Eichmann's eyes narrowed, and his teeth clenched as he paused. And how do you repay us? He stared deeply into each pair of eyes of the men who by now were cowering in his shadow. With slander! With lies and communist propaganda! He bellowed. The silence hung in the air like a blade atop a guillotine until Günther and then Rahm continued the harangue. Finally, with a nod from Eichmann, the artists' work was produced—three or four sketches and paintings created by each of the men who were buckling before their interrogators. Günther was particularly taken with a drawing by Haas entitled "Hunger" in which the Jews were depicted scavenging a pile of garbage in search of potato peelings. Each man except for Strass was ordered to identify the particular artwork he created.

Unable to look Günther in the eyes and humbling himself with sagging shoulders, Haas respectfully responded that he was merely making sketches of his surroundings as any artist would do. I am no communist, he uttered; I know nothing of politics…I'm a mere painter. But the questioning went on with the Germans demanding to know how the paintings were smuggled out and by whom. In response, the men could only shrug in ignorance.

Enough! Eichmann shrieked, now clearly frustrated with the apparent futility of the examination's purpose to uncover a sophisticated conspiracy—something specific that he could take back to Berlin. Haindl, who had been standing off to the side in deference to his superiors, stepped forward and let out his frustrations. Hauling off, he smashed his fist into Troller's face, forcing the man to stumble backwards.

"Into the cellar with you!" Haindl shouted, kicking the staggering Troller.

Other SS and Gestapo officers eagerly joined in slapping and kicking the men toward the basement door where they were pushed down the stairs into a dimly lit and frigid cellar. As their eyes adjusted to the dark surroundings, they were all drawn to a flicker of light coming from a small barred window above. Settling in, the six men sat in stony silence, preoccupied with their own thoughts.

Troller worried about mundane matters, not yet appreciating the seriousness of his circumstances. He fretted about possibly missing the date he had scheduled later that evening with his girlfriend. Would she be angry with him for not showing up? Would she agree to see him again? He was anxious about who would protect his sister in his absence. But despite these thoughts and a relatively calm appearance on the outside, Troller was struggling against the urge to vomit his guts out.

Not so with Ungar, who rocked to and fro, shaking with fits of hysterical crying. "We shall hang by evening! They are setting up the gallows now," he kept repeating, paying no attention to the distress this caused his fellow prisoners.

After a while, things calmed down, and the men engaged in whispered conversations interrupted sporadically by weeping. Will we be hanged? Sent to the Little Fortress? Tortured or beaten to death? No one had an answer. For several hours, they speculated over their future. Suddenly, the upstairs door was yanked open, and the heels of SS officers Moes and Günther snapped sharply down the flight of stairs.

Günther was the first to speak, doing so in a disarming, conciliatory tone. Who else are members in this communist ring of yours? Give us some names, and you will be set free, he promised, his twisted lips forming a sardonic smile. When nothing was forthcoming from the cringing men, the SS officer raised his voice considerably. Strass! Günther hollered. Who were your customers? Who bought the pictures? The men quaked in silence with confusion on their faces. They knew nothing of a communist plot. There were no names to furnish. They merely painted and sketched what they observed.

Moes's face grew beet red. He pulled his Luger from its holster, pointing the pistol at each man while screaming for answers. Still silence. In disgust, Moes and Günther turned on their heels and marched up the stairs with the door slamming shut behind them.

It had grown dark by that time, and the single ray of light shining through the lone window was gone. Even with their eyes adjusting to the darkness, the men could barely see their outstretched hands before them. A half hour had passed when suddenly

Fritta leaped up. He bolted to the window, pressing his ears to the opening; his body jerked in agitation; there were tears in his eyes. My son! He shrieked. It's him, he said, referring to the four-year-old lad; I can tell by his footsteps!

But the remote possibility of discerning one specific set of footsteps outside the window amidst the milling crowd of people that had been forming was made impossible with the roar of truck engines bellowing and the rumble of huge tires over the cobbled street. Moments later, brakes squealed as the trucks came to a halt; the motors were left idling, meaning the vehicles would not remain for long. Next came a clanging of keys at the basement's door, which burst open with Haindl bellowing, "Raus! Raus!" This was followed by a stampede of boots on the steps. The light emanating from the top of the stairway illuminated men accoutered in the uniforms of the SS carrying rifles.

Arms and fists flayed everywhere. The Germans grabbed and tugged at the cowering men and lifted them from their stooped positions, dragging them across the basement floor while kicking their torsos and striking their backs with rifle butts. The men's ears rang from the unrelenting shrieking of "Raus! Raus! Macht schnell!"

One by one, the men were led out of the building where SS guards were idly standing around several trucks with their motors grumbling for attention. The vehicles were covered with tarpaulin on all sides except for the rear, which was open and from which a short ladder hung, providing entrance to the interior.

Some people were already inside the trucks: Strass's frail wife and Troller's girlfriend (they would have their date together after all, though not in the way intended); the wives of Haas, Bloch, Ungar, and Fritta; even Fritta's young son, whose footsteps he had indeed recognized, and Ungar's five-year-old daughter. About five meters away, a group of the men's other relatives and friends and even people they did not know were waving at them, forcing smiles of encouragement; be brave, their faces seemed to say.

The men sat on the floors of the trucks in silence; that is, everyone but Ungar, who began to cry. A friendly voice arose from the gathering, whispering to whoever could hear, "If the truck turns left, it will mean Prague, and that can't be too bad. But if it turns right, it means the Little Fortress." The brakes were released, and the trucks slowly drove off, turning right.

The Little Fortress, as it was known because it was a miniature version of my exterior, was situated about a mile south of my outer walls, just over the Eger

Bridge. The mere mention of its name struck terror into the hearts of my people for few wearing the Jewish Star ever returned; almost all who entered died there or were dispatched to some other heinous place where they were likely murdered. Those inmates who were Russian prisoners of war fared somewhat better except when they were caught trying to escape, in which case they were shot or hanged.

Prior to being put to use by the Germans as a place of brutal punishment, the building had been a maximum security prison for long-term and common criminals. The edifice contained rows of dark dungeons carved out from subterranean casements, each holding about 200 prisoners. Heavy iron crossbars secured the doors of the cells with a small window above each door. Inside each casement, there was one water closet, one slimy washstand, and one iron coal stove. Every morning and night, the clanking of ancient wrought-iron padlocks being secured echoed off the walls.

Inside the casements, the inmates slept along the sidewalls in bunk beds that were hundreds of years old. Sometimes, it was just as well to sleep on the floor or if fortunate, a straw mattress. There might be a blanket or two, but one had to be careful that it was free of bedbugs and flees.

Making their way over a foul-smelling moat, the trucks screeched to a halt. "Raus! Raus!" bellowed two SS men waving their rifle butts. The Jews climbed out of the trucks. More SS guards surrounded the trembling group, screaming at the slightest move made by any of the arrivals who were ordered to face the exterior wall of the fortress. They were instructed not to make a sound or a move, and all complied except for the children, who cried incessantly.

The relentless sun burned down upon the wilting inmates, and the heat became overbearing. One man squinted over his shoulder and was immediately struck, knocked down, and kicked by the guards. More people joined the group; not all were Jews. Soon, the prisoners began swaying like sheaves of wheat while they struggled to remain erect outside the gate of the Little Fortress. Suddenly, the SS men barked more commands: Right! Left! Left! Right! The women and children were commanded to go right as they entered the Little Fortress, the men to go left.

A dozen names were called including the men of The Painters' Affair. The men stepped forward and were hustled into an office filled with two long tables, chairs, and a filing cabinet. A red-faced typist sat typing one finger at a time. Another man was holding a folder, and a third man looked at them and yawned. Then a command: "Answer questions quickly!" Name, parents' names, race, date of birth, birthplace, schools attended, profession, last residence…Sign! After several hours, the new arrivals were sent to their sleeping quarters.

Haas, Fritta, Troller, Bloch, Ungar and Strass were taken to a casement holding 100 men, all Jews. They were made to strip, empty buckets, and shower, after which they were deloused. Remnants of Czech army uniforms that were no more than rags were handed out. After the men put on the clothing, an SS man went down the line, and with a brush and pail of yellow paint in hand, he placed a stencil on each man's chest, painting a Jewish star over his heart and a yellow stripe on the side of his trousers.

SS men were assigned to serve as jailers to groups of prisoners. In the case of the men of The Painters' Affair, the jailer was an SS man named Stefan Rojko who thoroughly enjoyed his work, particularly when engaged in torturing, shooting, and hanging the prisoners. Rojko was typical of many of those who lorded over the inmates. After a day spent making life miserable for the prisoners with an occasional act of murder thrown in, Rojko returned home where he was greeted by his blond wife in her peasant dress scurrying back to the kitchen to finish preparing dinner. His two small children would stop whatever they were doing to stare up at their father gazing down at them with an air of munificence. To his children, Rojko appeared regal in his uniform with his military hat serving as a crown.

Seating himself at the head of a small table, Rojko took his time eating dinner, glancing up every so often to look around the tiny room as though it was a palace. While he behaved as any man might have who had put in an ordinary day's labor, inside he felt like a king having spent his day as an absolute ruler with the power of life and death over his subjects. Yet before the war, Rojko was a most common man working as a servant for a family in Styria, a village in Austria. He also served as the priest's helper and pulled the rope to ring the town's church bell. How did he transition from tugging a cathedral bell to yanking the noose around a Jew's neck?

Another example of less-than-exemplary behavior was the way some of my people took advantage of their superior positions vis-à-vis their fellow prisoners. Each cell had a designated commander, and in the case of the men of The Painters' Affair, the commander was a man named Adler whom no one trusted. Adler did not have to work, and it was assumed by everyone that he was a collaborator, clandestinely providing information to the German Authority. When the men were out, he stayed behind to steal every last crumb of bread he could lay his hands on. Adler was prone to having fits of shouting, and when he did, his eyes nearly detonated from their sockets. He was a thoroughly disgusting-looking man with greenish, pale skin, and his face was always unshaven. At the end of the war, his last group of cellmates strangled him with his own wire.

Sometimes, the prisoners were assigned real work either outside the Little Fortress in quarry pits or long-abandoned mine shafts or inside the prison's walls carting building material, mixing concrete, and setting iron doors. But for the most part, their days were spent enduring unabated torture from the sadistic guards. Inmates were forced to run with fully loaded wheelbarrows, and when they collapsed, which they invariably did, a sneering guard would scream at the quaking man lying on the ground frozen from fear, his arms upraised, vainly attempting to shield his face from the thrashing inflicted upon him. Older prisoners returning from the quarry pits were made to do calisthenics or run five times around the court as the amused guards flogged them with whips and bludgeoned them with sticks until they dropped. Such was the daily regimen that each prisoner looked forward to upon awakening to the dawn of a new day.

The men of The Painters' Affair could also count on more methodical forms of torture designed to elicit information. Amidst the pounding and kicking, questions were shouted. Who are your communist co-conspirators? Where are the rest of your paintings? Who smuggled this slanderous propaganda out from here? From whom did you receive your orders? Given there were no real answers to the fictitious conspiracy the Germans had concocted, the men could only accept their situation with resignation and silently endure the beating and shrieking inflicted upon them while waiting and hoping it would come to an end before they did.

Despite the fact the men of The Painters' Affair were arrested at the same time and essentially accused of identical crimes, they encountered different fates. After three months in the Little Fortress, Troller, an architect whose only drawings were mainly of children, was regarded as posing little threat and thus dispatched to Auschwitz where he somehow survived. After the war, Troller returned to my former domain, which had transformed itself into something quite the antithesis of what I had been. There were no crowded streets, no three-tier bunk beds with inmates crammed into stuffy, bug-infested quarters, no old people wandering aimlessly, no rampant dysentery or disease, no Nazi thugs, no transports. Indeed, as Troller walked through the town square filled with foliage and flowers, he blinked his eyes in disbelief, staring at his previous living quarters which had been transformed into an ordinary bakery the likes of which he could find in any village, town, or city.

Otto Ungar did not fare as well as Troller, although he too was shipped to Auschwitz. While Ungar took some solace knowing his wife and daughter were also released from the Little Fortress, he died unaware that they would be among my survivors.

Like Troller, Ungar was still alive when Auschwitz was abruptly abandoned by the Germans. In the knowledge that the war was in its waning days, the Germans desperately wanted to cover up all evidence of their crimes. Thus, on a particularly frigid predawn morning, thousands of barely breathing skeletons were driven from their barracks and ordered to form columns in preparation for the march to Germany. Slowly, the mass of humanity slogged its way out of the camp, beginning a horrific journey that would become known as The Death March, spanning hundreds of miles in frozen, tundra-like, snow-covered Europe.

Those few survivors who were not shot by the guards nor frozen nor starved to death along the journey were deposited in Buchenwald, where Ungar, barely alive, was liberated and taken to a small, bleak hospital eight miles away. Emaciated and shrunken from disease, Ungar finally succumbed, his contorted hand still clinging to the bed sheets, the same hand with which he created the drawings that landed him in so much trouble to begin with but which had been rendered useless for painting after the Nazis severed two of his fingers.

Felix Bloch eluded a prolonged and tortuous end to his life. Unable to endure the savage thrashings inflicted upon him, Bloch died only several days after his arrival at the Little Fortress. On the other hand, František Strass, who was already in his seventies, had a tremendous ability to absorb pain, and although beaten again and again, he remained defiant. Lying bloody and helpless on the ground with his legs battered numb, leaving him unable to move, Strass would glare into the eyes of whoever was striking him just daring the man to continue. We will see, Strass seemed to be saying, just who will tire first! After three months, he and his wife were shipped to Auschwitz where they both were gassed along with Dr. Karl Fleishmann.

For whatever reason, perhaps nothing more than an unfortunate expression or an insolent glance, poor Fritta aroused the animosity of the jailers almost from the start, setting them into a frenzy whenever he came into view. Like a pack of rabid dogs frothing at the mouth, they would pounce on Fritta who, unlike Strass, screamed and cried with each fisticuff and kick and lash of the whip or strike from a stick. As strong as he had been, it wasn't long before his body grew feeble as he staggered on wobbly legs with his shoulders slouching and arms drooping. Fritta, who had hardly ever been sick while in my domain, soon developed a case of dysentery which remained with him during his time in the Little Fortress.

Haas considered himself more fortunate than the others because after his arrival, he was separated from the rest of the men and sent to work in a factory. But even there, he was flogged every day, and soon he developed an infection on his leg. Most likely, without medicine, he would have died, but a fellow prisoner, Paul Wurzel, who fortuitously happened to be a doctor, used a rusty saw to cut away the infected area. Rendered unable to work, Haas was thrown into an underground cell where he was soon joined by Fritta.

Eventually, the Gestapo decided there was not much point in letting Fritta and Haas live. Bloch was already dead, and Strass, Ungar, and Troller had been shipped to Auschwitz. One day, after shivering in the subterranean cell, the two men were summoned to appear for a hearing. Perhaps the Germans had come to their senses and realized this was all a misunderstanding, and they would be released, the two men likely hoped. Led to an office, their hearts sank when they saw SS Captain Hans Günther seated before them, scratching his red neck just above the stiff collar of his uniform. With bravado and fanfare, Günther read an indictment informing the men that they were charged with perpetrating horror propaganda against the Reich, and a warrant had been issued for their arrest.

You both must sign the document, Günther instructed, handing each man a pen but making sure there was no unintended brushing of fingers, as though the Jews quaking before him were lepers, and he would contract their disease. Ungar and Troller affixed their names as they were ordered. Formalities being satisfied, the men were led back to their cell. The next day, they were herded onto a freight car bound for Auschwitz.

Fritta was only thirty-five at the time, but from the constant beatings, his youthful, robust body was merely a frail shadow of its former self; Fritta might as well have been a withered, weary man of eighty for all the strength he still retained. Though eight years older, Haas carried the limp torso of his friend to the pail secreted in the corner of the freight car which served as the common toilet for the passengers on their way to Auschwitz. Because of Fritta's dysentery, this was necessitated several times an hour. The stench was overpowering, and it wasn't long before there was no distinction between the stink from the bucket and the odor Fritta bore.

Immediately after the freight train pulled into Auschwitz, Fritta was sent straight to the infirmary. He was clearly unable to work and too ill to even walk to the "showers" so he was condemned to languish until he met his death. When visiting him, Haas and Troller could only hope that Fritta recognized them since the best he could muster was a turn of the lips in a poor imitation of a smile. But with no reason for living, Fritta gave up, and eight days after his arrival at Auschwitz, Bedrich "Fritta" Taussig was dead.

Haas made out better. Shortly after Fritta's death in August 1944, Haas was sent to Sachsenhausen, and because of his artistic abilities, he was assigned to a counterfeiting unit. His job was to create plates that could be used to print currency that would pass muster for the British pound sterling. Thus being useful to the Germans, Leo Haas survived and was liberated in May 1945. His wife also survived, and together, they adopted Fritta's young son, Thomas.

Haas did more than rescue little Thomas from the remains of my domain. After the war, he returned to my former realm just as Troller had done. It was like paying a respectful visit to a cemetery and somberly pondering the buried corpses of the dead beneath the headstones, except when Haas and Troller made their visits, there were no defining markers or any signs that those who had died within my walls had ever existed in the first place. Haas was overcome with the sheer ordinariness of the surroundings. The streets and buildings were filled with people going about their common activities, looking just like any city Haas had seen. Would people even believe what had happened here? Would people overcome the difficulty conceiving that some humans could be so cruel and vicious to other humans? That there could be such a vast amount of suffering never acknowledged by the rest of the world even when my gates were open for inspection?

Haas had the answer. With deliberate steps, he made his way, never once doubting the path to his destination. There...there, where he had hidden his work; it seemed to be a lifetime ago. Leo Haas's trembling yet resolute hands removed the paintings that would bear testimony to the world and serve as witness on behalf of all my people.

CHAPTER ELEVEN: LIBERATION

On October 28, 1944, a train clattered over the tracks, carrying those unfortunate enough to comprise the final ensemble of deportees destined for the dreaded East. To make the matter even more heart wrenching, all of my remaining young people were included in this final group along with the artists who had not been selected for transport in the previous two weeks. There was one exception, however—Mariánka Zadikow, who had been nineteen when she first walked through my gates. And what act of providence spared her a probable death at the end of the line? Clerical error and nothing more. Such was the manner in which the hand of fate dealt the cards in my world.

Day after day in the following six months, Mariánka witnessed the same scene of starving survivors from the death camps trudging under my archway. Inside my environs, they would join the ravenous 11,000 inhabitants who were already scrambling amongst themselves, wolfing down the smallest scrap of stale bread or rotting victuals but like squirrels, stowing a portion for later just in case they would live long enough to need it. Human optimism is something that has never ceased to impress me.

Remaining on hand to reluctantly welcome the daily influx of Jews from the camps was a populace comprised of German and Austrian Jews over sixty-five or disabled from World War I, all the Danish Jews, a handful of Czech Jews, Jews with one gentile parent or married to a gentile spouse, and the Dutch prominents. As a public relations ploy, Himmler himself negotiated to trade 1,200 of my people in exchange for five million in Swiss francs put up by several Jewish organizations. On

February 5, 1945, 523 German Jews, 433 Dutch Jews, 153 Austrian Jews, and 91 Jews from the Protectorate reached Switzerland and freedom. The Germans were meticulous even at the end. The numbers totaled 1,200 exactly.

My appearance underwent a strange transformation in the early months of 1945. With so many elderly joined by the constant influx of survivors from the killing camps and death marches, conditions rapidly deteriorated. The smell of unclean clothing and unwashed bodies was prevalent, the odor of death even more so. People wandered aimlessly with little to do but wait out the uncertainty that lay ahead. Everyone knew the war's end was near, and the outcome was clear, but their fate was far from certain. Would they live to see my gates open, allowing them to exit without hindrance? And if so, to what end?

In the midst of this purgatory, once again the Germans presented their heinous face of deceit, creating a theater of the absurd for the rest of humanity to observe. I would be the main character of the play, assigned the task to convince the world that whatever would be discovered at the other camps was the exception, and the true treatment of the Jews by the Germans could be learned from me. Always the one for showmanship and knowing the war's conclusion was rapidly approaching, Himmler turned to his trusted and reliable subordinate who had accomplished so much in executing the Reich's policy toward the Jews, Adolph Eichmann, directing him to craft a stage and arrange for an inspection by the Red Cross of my environs.

And so it came to pass that on April 5, 1945, in his freshly pressed and starched gray uniform, though appearing gaunt in the face which caused his nose to protrude and jaw to thrust forward even more than usual, Adolph Eichmann forced a smile as he welcomed M. Paul Donant of the Swiss Red Cross. Leading him by the elbow, Eichmann escorted Donant through my streets, squares, and buildings that had been scrubbed and cleaned earlier in the morning. The tour was well planned with Eichmann exuding confidence, knowing that Donant would see only what the Germans wanted him to see and nothing else.

To ensure that Donant would file the report the Germans desired, an elaborate formal reception was held that evening in the Hradschin Palace in Prague. The tables sparkled with silver and creamy linen. Food and drinks were in abundance. Lieutenant General Karl Frank, Protector for Bohemia and Moravia, hosted the event. Rising regally from his chair, Frank cleared his throat to address the guests. His hawkish nose moved like a pointer as he focused on portions of the room. Lieutenant General Frank welcomed everyone while offering a special nod and smile for the guest of honor, M. Paul Donant.

Hans Frank, whose fleshy face, receding hairline, and beady eyes were in stark contrast to Lieutenant General Frank to whom he bore no relation, rose to share witty stories with those assembled. As Hitler's personal lawyer and the Reich's foremost jurist, Hans Frank could not have been more charming as he toasted Donant with champagne while a pianist played Chopin. Though they had no relatives in common, what Karl and Hans Frank did share was a similar fate; in a year, each would be hanging dead at the end of a rope.

Ten days later, a convoy of Swedish buses arrived to evacuate the remaining 423 Danish Jews. Commandant Rahm and Assistant Commandant Haindl lumbered to the embarkation area to observe. Haindl, accoutered in a pressed, black uniform and chomping on a cigar, looked on derisively. Raising one booted foot onto the running board of a bus, Haindl began to climb aboard to speak to one of the evacuees when the bus driver told him bluntly, "You cannot come aboard. You are on international territory." Dumbstruck and seething, Haindl hesitated and then backed down the steps, struggling to regain his lost dignity. No longer was his every word a command from on high to be unquestionably obeyed. No longer did he hold the power of life and death over so many. The tide had turned. Two days later, Rahm gathered the remaining 20,000 inmates and addressed them in a way that would have been inconceivable only weeks earlier.

"Meine Herren," he began...

Events moved swiftly. Like the onslaught of a hurricane, wave after wave of survivors from other camps arrived. Things were so chaotic that I doubt even the Germans with their aptitude for exactness could have maintained an accurate count. From April 20 to May 2, somewhere between 13,500 and 15,000 barely breathing, skeletal shadows slogged into my milieu. Many of these wretched souls were Polish Jews coming from Buchenwald while the rest came from other eastern concentration camps and death marches. Once again, my streets teemed with human bodies, more than 30,000 drifting apparitions, barely alive, seeking morsels of food, something to drink, and a place to lie down and sleep. These survivors also brought with them typhus, setting off an epidemic. Ironically, the Germans tried to control its spread by killing the body lice that caused the disease with Zyklon B, the same chemical they used killing Jews in the gas chambers. Lice…Jews…what difference did it make to the Germans?

Sensing the time had come, Commandant Rahm abdicated, and on May 3, the Red Cross flag was raised. With his eyes rising upward as the banner ascended the pole, one of my people, Carl Meinhard, who had been a theater producer in Berlin, swore an oath I shall always remember: Theresienstadt, ever to forget; that would be nearly as much a crime as this one.

Over the next several days, Rahm and the remaining SS attachment gathered their belongings and fled my domain like rats leaving a sinking ship. Though out of sight, the Germans were not out of earshot. Scurrying past my walls, the SS were confronted by the advancing Soviet army. The SS men, joined by some scattered German military, fought for a path through a battlefield, hoping to make it back to Berlin. Less than two days later, the air was still and silent. The fighting had ceased, and on May 9, Soviet troops marched over my cobbled streets.

With the Germans gone, attention focused on combating the typhus that was rapidly proliferating throughout the population. Fortunately, the weather was becoming milder, making it easier to endure delousing. People washed however they could, and the clothes of those stricken were burned. But despite the valiant effort, complete containment was not possible, and hundreds of my people died on a daily basis.

On May 11, accompanying the arrival of more Soviet Army units was a medical team to battle the typhus epidemic. Those Jews well enough and with a destination in mind departed from my domain. Mariánka Zadikow and her mother joined the stream of Jews pouring down the road leading away from my ramparts. Making their way in the opposing direction, the original Christian population began to trickle back to their former homes.

Others, like Ludwig and Sophie Frank, would wait until dispatched to a displaced persons camp, which in their case was the Bavarian city of Deggendorf that had its own distinctive history with the Jews. In the fourteenth century, most of the Jews of Deggendorf were slaughtered to extinguish debt owed to them by the town's populace. Now these Jewish survivors of the camps were relocated to heal their wounds at a site where a similar carnage had once been committed against their ancestors. How little had changed.

• • •

A corporeal entity gives little thought to the cells that composite its body, but with me, it is different. Each individual human who at one time or another became a part of my essence mattered beyond words. Hence, their numbers are of little consequence, and yet, the numbers are needed to complete my story. Despite the German obsession for record keeping and my own memory of each individual, exactitude is elusive. About 140,000 Jews, at one time or another, inhabited my realm from November 1941 until April 1945. The average population was 40,000 despite the fact the buildings within my ramparts were constructed to house no more than 7,000. A little more than half of the Jews, something between 74,000 and 76,000, were Czech; the rest were German (42,000), Austrian (15,000), and from other countries.

Of my people, 33,430 died within my walls; a few were executed, but most succumbed as the result of beatings, exhaustion, disease, and starvation. About 87,000 inmates were transported to Auschwitz and other camps where 95% of them died. Of the 20,000 survivors when the Red Cross flag was raised above my ramparts, a quarter expired within weeks from typhus. Thus I, the model of the camps, the Paradise Ghetto and proof to the world of how well Hitler treated his Jews, was a place where once you entered, the chances were nine in ten you would soon die one way or another.

Yet most heart wrenching of all and even more incomprehensible to me was what was perpetrated upon my children—all 15,000 young, upturned faces with every reason in the world to be brightly staring into the future, anticipating a long life lying ahead. But instead, luminous eyes turned dull; playfulness transformed into weariness, laughter into tears, sprightly steps into plodding, life into death. Fifteen thousand youngsters strode under my archway; 150 survived.

Those first days of freedom from the Germans remain a maze in my mind. While my streets were once again surging with swarms of human figures, unlike before when my people trudged their way through the congestion, this time the pace was frenetic and purposeful with heads held high and eyes cast forward in expectation of something better. Those providing aid were determined to halt the spread of death once and for all. This much was evident from the way their shoulders squared, their voices exuded resolve, their instructions spoken with confidence.

Within my populace, nationalities abounded and were more diverse than ever. The German, Austrian, Czech, and Polish Jews were soon joined by Swiss, Danish, and Russian Jews. But it was the first American to arrive whom I shall never forget and who never forgot me, a man who lingers in my mind's eye to this day.

Forty-year-old Meyer Levin was born and raised in Chicago. As a reporter and magazine editor, film critic and author, he was charged with making documentary films for the U.S. Office of War Information. Eventually, he became a war correspondent for the Jewish Telegraphic Agency, and it was in this capacity and tasked with the mission of uncovering the fate of the survivors of the concentration camps that Levin came face-to-face with me.

I noticed him at once as he approached my gates in his Jeep; the fluttering of a small red, white, and blue American flag was something I had never seen before. He was staring stoically straight ahead with his round face and bulbous nose while making his way through my portico, totally unprepared for what he was about to witness.

The Jeep slowed to a crawl, torturously traversing the teeming streets, moving in fits and starts to avoid hitting pedestrians. Finally, it emerged from the crowds when forced to a halt by lines of my people awaiting the daily ration of bread. Levin looked on as an open truck attempted to drive through the multitude to deliver the bread for distribution. First one, then another, and in moments, a throng of emaciated and ravenous survivors clamored on the sides of the vehicle, creating a cacophony of metallic clanks in the air. Ignoring shouts for order from the Jewish police, the mob pressed forward in an effort to reach the truck. Levin had lived through the Depression, but never had he witnessed such a thing.

Levin was taken aback by what he saw that day. At the other camps he visited, he had an idea what to expect, although he was still shaken to the core seeing the piles of corpses rising six, eight, and even ten feet into the flea-infested air, the clusters of gaunt stick figures barely standing and staring at him through sunken eyes. He struggled to avoid averting his eyes while he compelled them to remain open like the shutter of a camera, blinking and photographing the vision for posterity. But still, he could not help throwing his head back to avoid the assault from the stench of rotting flesh.

However, Levin expected me to be different. After all, wasn't he informed that I was Hitler's Paradise Ghetto and a city for the Jews? It did not take Levin long to realize otherwise.

The reek of death from typhus was everywhere while the Jewish medical staff and Red Cross fought to turn the tide against the dreaded disease. Those who could walk wandered the streets and alleys like specters floating over the ground with nowhere to go. Levin had seen other camps and believed that in the end, the human spirit would prove victorious over death, and the survivors would slowly rejoin the world of the living even though they never would be made completely whole or be the same as they were before.

Nor would Levin. He would do what writers do and write novels about Jews in concentration camps and their struggles to adjust to life after liberation. He would become obsessed with the diary of Anne Frank and pen a play about it. He would move to Palestine and make a film concerning a child-survivor searching for his family in the nascent Jewish homeland. He would join the Jewish underground fighting to establish the Jewish state that would become Israel.

But this and much more was in his future. When it was time to depart, Levin's Jeep retraced its path through my archway and into the open air, leaving the throngs of pressing flesh and the aroma of stale breath behind. Craning his neck, Levin took one last look at the camp that was known to him as Theresienstadt.

Unbeknownst to Levin, at that very moment, he was witnessing my transmutation as I abandoned the corporeal world. The mortar and stones, the concrete and bricks, the dirt and grass, the trees and shingles would all remain in my wake just as they were before I was summoned into being. To the naked eye, there would be nothing different to the edifice I once was for my brief time on earth. But something did not remain, which I took with me.

The collective soul of those who were my people was retained in my phantasmal essence both for the present and for the future. This was something that could no longer be altered. It was who and what I was and who and what I am, floating through the sea of space, drifting down the tide of time, not just a mere memory but a living reality to be encountered for those who seek me out.

EPILOGUE

During the months following liberation, the green leaves firmly hanging from the branches of the trees surrounding the walls of the Czechoslovakian town of Terezín began to lose their grip as they transformed into yellow, orange, and brown hues. September of 1945 had arrived, and in front of the Little Fortress, a national cemetery was founded. A year later, sober faces uttered somber words and conducted a funeral over the remains of my people found in mass graves; a memorial service was held, marking the beginning of a tradition of solemn annual ceremonies. The fact that virtually all of those who perished at *Terezín* were Jews was disregarded by the Communist regime that preferred to remember all victims of racial and political persecution; that this was motivated more by Jew-hating than any desire to promote the oneness of humanity I do not doubt.

In the late sixties, a library with archives, photos, and trained docents was established, informing inquisitive visitors just what this seemingly pleasant town had been like a quarter of a century earlier. Twenty years later, when the Communist regime collapsed, the Ghetto Museum in Terezín was created. The crematorium was reconditioned and opened to the public so those who were interested could see for themselves where the remains of 50,000 Jews had been reduced to ashes.

Atop an expansive, well-maintained lawn where the grass presented itself as one continuous carpet of brilliant green in the spring and summer months, rectangular, gray stone markers were set in rows constituting the Jewish Cemetery where more than 9,000 bodies had been buried. A silver Star of David, eight feet high, loomed over the burial ground, pronouncing to those who paid a visit that the graveyard's denizens were not heterogeneous citizens of the world but a people who died because they were Jews.

It has been some time now—years, decades, millennia; past, present, future; all the same to me—since I inhabited a corporeal form. No longer am I restricted to stones and mortar occupying a specific spot on earth. The feeling is exhilarating to say the least, to be able to move about without restraint, bound by nothing, and being nowhere and everywhere at the same time. But make no mistake, I am just as alive as the day I was birthed, and other than lacking a physical structure, I am very much the same as I always have been and always will be.

Except for my composition, that is. My bones and organs do not consist of concrete and timber, nor foliage and human flesh—nothing that can be touched and felt nor smelt and seen. Like an amorphous cloud floating invisibly beyond the heavens, here, there, and everywhere, my constitution now belongs to another dimension. Yet, I can be easily understood and accessed by anyone who wishes to do so.

This is because I am now nothing more than memory, and it is memory of which I am composed, and it is memory through which I can be reached. I am the memory of every one of my people who occupied a place, no matter how small, and lived for a time, no matter how brief, within me when I was a physical entity on the human landscape. I am the memory of every person who recounts my whole story or the tiniest portion thereof. I am the memory of anyone who inquires after me and learns something about me. I am the memory of those yet to be who will seek me out. So long as there is a memory of me, even if only the slightest recollection of a single person, I am alive.

This, then, is the conclusion of my memoir.

Except, that is, for one final story.

• • •

One day, a letter dated July 1945 arrived in a mailbox belonging to a woman of twenty-five living in Philadelphia, Pennsylvania. The missive issued by the German Jewish Representative Committee was, for the most part, a form letter with some specific individualized information inserted. The dark-haired woman had been fluent in English even before she fled Germany eight years earlier so she had no difficulty reading the letter as her blazing, brown eyes darted back and forth over the page.

Dear Friends:

We are happy to inform you that we have just received from the offices of The World Jewish Congress in London a message for the daughter living in Philadelphia that Ludwig Frank and Sophie Frankhas [sic] *been found among the survivors of Theresienstadt.*

If no address has been mentioned above, we are sorry that it is not possible, for the time being, to get in touch with your relatives liberated in Theresienstadt.

Ruth's hands were trembling, and she could barely hold on to the letter. Unbeknownst to Ruth, her parents were safe and secure in D. P. Center Deggendorf, and eventually, arrangements would be made for them to reunite with her and her older sister, Irma. Upon arriving in the States, Ludwig and Sophie would also greet their first grandchild, Irma's daughter, who was born in 1943, and after moving in with Ruth and her husband, they would be present for the birth of their first grandson.

I had spoken about a watch belonging to Ludwig when I recounted how the German Jews arrived; it was a silver pocket watch Ludwig was permitted to keep after the Germans seized his gold watch that was a family heirloom handed down from one generation to the next. In lieu of the confiscated timepiece, Ludwig had hoped that one day he'd be able to pass on the silver substitute to a grandson for a bar mitzvah present. And though Ludwig planned on doing so, he died several years before his eldest grandson reached the age of thirteen.

However, the watch did make its way to Ludwig's oldest grandson soon after his bar mitzvah, and he was pleased because he remembered his Opa very well. After all, he grew up with his mother's parents and even lived with them under the same roof the first seven years of his life. He could never forget how often this kindly old man with sparkling bluish-gray eyes would tug on a chain and withdraw the tarnished watch from his vest pocket, holding it out, saying that it would be his on his bar mitzvah.

Ludwig's grandson kept the watch in a small, white box with a rubber band around it so it would not fall out. When he married and moved into a home of his own to start his own family, he took the watch with him and placed the box in a drawer with a few other sentimental possessions. After several years, the watch beckoned, and he commissioned a jeweler to design a small stand in the form of a branchless tree on which to set the timepiece. At the base of the tree, the name Ludwig Frank was inscribed in a flow of interlacing letters. Ludwig's grandson wrote about the watch and its story, and the essay was published, encouraging its author to write more, which he did.

Decades later, when Ludwig's grandson was approaching the age his grandfather had been as he trudged beneath my archway for the first time, and I was in need of a mortal to scribe my tale, I approached Richard, seeking his assistance. There was no need for anything to be said; words, spoken or written, are not within my capacity in any event. Yet, a pact was struck just the same.

Richard became my ghostwriter, transcribing my memoir. At times, the work was arduous for I am a difficult and elusive subject. But he held up his part of the bargain to my satisfaction.

For my part, there was nothing I had to do that I hadn't been doing already, no need to perform any task out of the ordinary whatsoever. As with so many others, I have been with Richard all his life and will be for his remaining days. Ironically, I have been his ghost just as he has been mine, haunting him like a persistent mist seeping into the skin and soul, a relentless spirit that won't let go.

And even if I decided to vanish like some specter in the night, granting him tranquility and freedom from the memory of me, it would not matter. Richard would still remain haunted by me. He would have it no other way, which is as it should be for Richard and for the rest of humankind, as well.

About the Author

Richard D. Bank, Esq. is the author of eight books including *The Everything Judaism Book*, T*he Everything Guide to Writing Nonfiction*, and *Feig*, a novel. He is a past president and current board member of the Philadelphia Writers' Conference. Richard has published over 100 articles, essays, short stories and book reviews and has taught writing courses at the University of Pennsylvania, Temple University and other venues. He is on the faculty of Rosemont College in the MFA and Graduate Publishing programs where he teaches creative nonfiction and publishing law. A lifelong resident of the Philadelphia area, Richard lives in Upper Dublin with his wife Francine.

CPSIA information can be obtained
at www.ICGtesting.com
Printed in the USA
BVOW06s2241100417
480900BV00003B/3/P